Out and About
in New Brunswick

by
Hank Deichmann

with illustrations by
Dodie Clark

DREAMCATCHER BOOKS & PUBLISHING
Saint John • New Brunswick • Canada

Canadian Cataloguing in Publication Data

Deichmann, Hank - 1934

Out and About in New Brunswick

ISBN 1-894372-33-6
     1. Animals--New Brunswick--Guidebooks. 2. Plants--New Brunswick--Guidebooks. I. Clark, Dodie II. Title.

QH106.2.N4D43 2004   578'.09715'1   C2004-905930-0

Editor: Yvonne Wilson

Typesetter: Chas Goguen

Illustrations: Dodie Clark

Cover Design: John van der Woude

Printed and bound in Canada

DREAMCATCHER BOOKS
& PUBLISHING INC.
105 Prince William Street
Saint John, New Brunswick
Canada E2L 2B2
1-877-631-READ
info@dreamcatcherbooks.ca

www.dreamcatcherbooks.ca

Dedication

The author is pleased and proud to dedicate this modest book to his immediate family, namely my wife Joanne, our two daughters, Jocelyn and Kirsten, and son Mark. Also included in the dedication is my mother Erica Matthiesen Deichmann/Gregg, and as of 2004 the following grandchildren, starting with youngest: Skylar, Thor, Reuben and Johan.

Geographically, our family and friends are located from the Atlantic to Pacific in Canada, and in the following states: California, Montana, Florida, Maryland and Massachusetts. Now across the Atlantic, Norway, Sweden, Denmark and the U.K. Again further afield, Kenya, Uganda, R.S.A. and India.

Acknowledgements

Over the last 60 years or so, give or take a few, I've been fortunate to be friends with, or work with, some mighty fine folks. I thank the people of the Kingston Peninsula, where I spent my early years. Also, I remember kindly those that I worked with both in industry and various levels of government in Newfoundland, Nova Scotia, Ontario, British Columbia and in my native New Brunswick. A speical thank you to the readers of the three weekly papers I contribute to: the "KV Weekend", the "King's County Weekend", and the "Charlotte County Weekend". Your feedback is always appreciated.

Last but not least, I **deeply** and **sincerely** thank Yvonne Wilson, my editor at DreamCatcher Publishing, and Chas Goguen, typesetter, who was instrumental in this project. It's fair to say that this book would never have seen the light of day if it hadn't been for their expertise and great patience.

Preface

As a small child, growing up in rural New Brunswick, Henrik (Hank) Deichmann spent countless hours traversing the fields, woods and shores of the Kingston Peninsula. While Hank absorbed the beauty of his surroundings, he was left with an insatiable curiosity about how these natural systems worked. In his search for answers, Hank pursued a variety of outdoor-oriented careers. Most notably, Hank held the positions of Chief Interpreter and Ecologist with Parks Canada in the Atlantic Region where he and his staff were able to spread the joy of nature to tens of thousands of people each year through a variety of park programs.

More recently, his writings have been found in a number of regional newspapers and outdoor journals and he has gained a considerable following. This book, with its down-home style of writing, will be welcomed by all who are interested in going beyond the sometimes dry details found in popular field guides. Hank's take on nature and the way he shares this information with the reader is the mark of a great nature interpreter, providing enough details to both inform and entertain, yet not bogging the reader down with overwhelming amounts of material.

Whether it's Deichmann's late spring stroll in the field with his grandson Thor, or his olfactory-based description of whale watching in the Bay of Fundy, Hank rekindles our natural childhood curiosity with his prose to ensure even the most ardent of city slickers will take the time to "smell the rugosas" on their next outing in the wilds or semi-wilds of New Brunswick.

Kelly P. Honeyman
Naturalist, J.D. Irving, Ltd.

Table of Contents

Map of New Brunswick

Major Towns and Cities

1. Setting the Stage

First we start with the foundation – the rocks. The most senior rocks in the Maritimes are in the order of 1.0 billion plus years old. Some of these rocks and many more are exposed around the city of Saint John, making a geologist's paradise. Oldest of the old are the ones of pre-Cambrian origin. These formations can be cheek by jowl with rocks that are much younger, or in the 200 million range. So, in the relatively small area encompassed by the city, with a bit of sleuthing one could very well find rocks with a great range in age, and in considerable variety.

Much of the city is based on *limestone*, as noted in names like Lime Kiln Road. Red Head is composed of *red sandstone*, and is youthful and, sadly for folks with houses at risk, unstable. The *granites* of Rockwood Park are in the middle range of age, or about 4 to 500 million years before present (B.P.).

As we go east in New Brunswick, particularly around Moncton and Petitcodiac, we find the landscape is less varied, a reflection of a more uniform geology. The sandstone formations in this area are of Pennsylvanian age or younger, making them "new kids" on the block, coming in at around 200 million years B.P.

Heading west, much of inland Charlotte is granite and related rocks. Grand Manan is unique in that the shore facing the rest of New Brunswick consists of columnar *basalt* cliffs. Very scenic and picturesque.

North to Fredericton and area, we run into the same type of *greywacke sandstone* formation as found in the neighbourhood of Moncton and the nearby coast of Kouchibouquac National Park.

Discussing the tremendous, rushing, giant tides of our Bay of Fundy (the highest or among the highest in all the world) a friend of mine expressed the opinion that it was too bad that the rocks and the tides of the upper Bay were a poor combination for durability: strong currents and soft rocks! The labels give a hint: *sandstone*, *siltstone*, even *mudstone*. Re-combined, or *conglomerate*, is about the strongest and even it succumbs to the relentless scouring. If you make regular visits to Fundy National Park, or Cape Enrage to the east, you'll see a difference from one season to the next, the erosion is so significant. "They don't make things like they used to!" There are some benefits though: the beautiful sea caves of St. Martins; numerous stacks, like Squaw Cap on the Fundy Park Shore; and finally the world famous Hopewell Rock Flowerpots. The Flowerpots literally "blow you away!"

Glaciation:

None of our province escaped the episodes of past glaciations. This is nowhere more obvious than in the Central Highlands. *Mount Carleton*, our highest peak (2,689 feet), is the centre piece of a park by the same name. It and its "peers," like *Mt. Elizabeth*, are made of strong stuff: *granite* and *rhyolite*.

The last ice of the most recent cold period was still melting a mere blink in geological time ago, 12,000 years B.P. The direction of the moving ice has been recorded in the alignment of hills and in the long dimension of lakes. Generally this trend is northeast to southwest.

Many areas that have been cleared for farming show glacial features. Oddly placed knolls in a jumble may represent *moraines* or *kame fields*. Cigar-shaped, abrupt hills may turn out to be *drumlins*. Drumlins often attract local names, like "whale's back," or "hog's back," quite descriptive. All these features can regularly be found along *river valleys* like the *Kennebecasis* and the *Magaguadavic*.

Rivers of gravel, a.k.a. *eskers*, are relatively rare in New Brunswick.

Fresh Water:

My Dad, a Scandinavian immigrant, used to try to help us children understand our Canadian heritage by explaining things simply. I heard him comment at one point that New Brunswick was one of the best watered regions in the world.

Over the years I have tested this comment a number of times. Major *rivers* in southern New Brunswick alone total about two dozen, and I know from personal experience that to take a tramp of any distance, one will cross a *brook* or two. Our largest *lake* is "Grand," at 65 square miles. It is south and east of Fredericton and hydrologically an integral part of the flow of the main St. John River. Going down river we find several sheets of water that, because of their size and reduced current, act like lakes. Examples are the *Washademoak*, *Belleisle Bay*, *Long Reach*, and *Kennebecasis Bay*. Other than Charlotte County and that part of Saint John County just east of the city there is a lack of small permanent lakes in this part of the Province. Generally, though, Dad had it right.

It seems that it rains or snows, or both, at least once a week here for an average of about 4 inches of precipitation per month year round. About 20% of the annual amount of falling weather arrives as snow. At the top of the province the ratio of snow to rain is much more in favour of the snow. This is important to the south as the accumulated snow pack powers the annual spring *flood*, universally in New Brunswick called the *freshet*. The peak on the Saint John River reaches

Fredericton the third week in April most years. It seems that there's always a *freshet*, and about every 20 springs there's a whopper.

Forest:
The valiant efforts of the European pioneers in the big land-clearing push of the early to the mid-1800's have largely been nullified by a reinvasion of the forest. In recent decades man has made his mark on the landscape mostly by large cut blocks as the province comes close to harvesting the annual increment of the forest. As to the pioneers, their work has been preserved in stone piles, amazingly persistent cedar rail fences, crumbling dwellings and barns, cellar holes. Lonely *apple trees*, and seemingly out of place *lilac bushes*, *delphiniums*, and *day lilies* testify to the dedication of long-gone pioneer women.

Farms:
As elsewhere, farms now are fewer and bigger, and are generally restricted to the best agricultural soils. Major truck-farming communities inland are based on the intervale meadows of *Maugerville*, *Sheffield*, and *Jemseg*. Deep *loams* allow profitable farming in sections of *Gagetown*, *Queenstown*, *Sussex* and the *Petitcodiac valley*, *Upham*, and *Hammondvale*. New Brunswick potato country is in the northwestern part of the Province: *Grand Falls*, *Perth-*

Andover, *Hartland* and *Woodstock*, based on sedimentary and calcium-based rocks. The *Shepody* area along the lower *Petiticodiac*, and the *Dorchester-Sackville* regions have benefited from *salt marshes*, that were reclaimable, and deposits of *marine clays*. These areas tend to lean towards *hay* growing and *pasturage* in lieu of the field crops favoured inland.

Landscape:

The diverse landscape of New Brunswick is a product of geology, moulded by *glaciation*, eroded by *rain* and *tides*, modified by *man*, and often clothed by a great variety of *trees*. It's beautiful! Many residents returning from travel to far off lands remark how appealing they find the view in their native land. Having been around Scandinavia a bit, my impression is that we're not as rugged as most of Norway, or as pastoral as Denmark, but a lot like southern Sweden; and I have heard from my Scots friends that we resemble in some ways the land of "auld lang syne."

sources; The N.B. Map Book, The Last Billion Years- Atlantic Geoscience Society.

2. A Cast of Characters

Plants:
Wild Flowers:

Hundreds of different *mosses* and *lichens* appear on the landscape. Only a few have common names. Most species of *clubmosses* and their relatives the *ferns* have common names, and a few people are able to discriminate among the different kinds. *Bracken* is our only dry-land fern; all the other 30 species or so like shade or dampness, or both. The four largest and most obvious to the casual observer are the *royal*, the *cinnamon*, the *interrupted*, and the *ostrich fern* or *fiddlehead*.

Many of our native plants are what botanists call vernal; they flower in the spring. The very earliest flower to appear is the dandelion-like *coltsfoot*. It's an import, and adjectives such as noxious, alien, and weed do actually fit. But the fact remains, it's first! Some years it appears in southern New Brunswick on south-facing banks by early March. Native wildflowers, like the *trout lily*, appear in earlier springs by late April, still a month behind the coltsfoot. The goal of these early bloomers is to go as far along with the annual development as possible before the trees above start to shade the forest floor with their unfurling leaves.

Northern- and southern-latitude flora meet in New Brunswick. Cool bogs are fine havens for northern type plants like *orchids*. South-facing hardwood stands with rich soils allow *wild ginger, bloodroot, Dutchman's breeches*, and *hepatica* to penetrate farther north than they otherwise would. New Brunswick has about 1,000 species of flowers in total, including established exotics or aliens.

Trees:
For our latitude we are richly endowed with about 90 species of trees and shrubs. This figure includes around 30 species of actual trees and about twice as many shrubs. European localities with similar climates as ours have about one half as many kinds of trees. It seems that in the New World the Appalachians, trending north and south, didn't inhibit tree movement north from the refugiums after the glacial ice melt, whereas the Alps and the Pyrenees in Europe were a barrier. Even compared to our neighbours in Nova Scotia we have a rich forest variety. *Northern white*

cedar, extremely rare in Nova Scotia, is widespread in New Brunswick, and we have a few trees that, while restricted and local in New Brunswick, are absent except as man-planted in Nova Scotia; the *basswood*, the *butternut*, and the *bur white oak* are in this category.

Animals:
Insects:
Arthropods: Worms and those who eat them:
New Brunswick has lots of different kinds of *insects*,

tens of thousands!! To them add hundreds of kinds of *arthropods*: *spiders* and *pill bugs*, *sowbugs*, *millipedes* and *centipedes*, and assorted *worms*, and the like.

Most of the larger earthworm varieties were unintentional introductions. They came in the soil adhering to plants brought from overseas. On this dietary supplement *moles*, *shrews*, *woodcocks* and *robins* thrive. The original worms - that is, the native species - are quite small and not a great food source.

Amphibians and Reptiles:
In the Maritmes there's only one *toad*, the garden variety. *Frogs* and *salamanders* have at least a dozen kinds

between them. The rarest frog is the *gray tree frog*. By far the biggest is the *bullfrog*; a big one can weigh a kilo!

Several of the *salamanders* are so well camouflaged and small that they are not often seen, and some (our largest, the *spotted*, among them) except for spawning live underground most of the year.

We have three kinds of *turtles*, ranging from the scary *snapping* kind to the quiet little *painted*. Old "red legs," a.k.a. the *wood turtle*, which spends many of its days wandering under hardwoods near water, is found over most of the province. The wood turtle is so pleasant in disposition that it's popular as a pet, which doesn't aid in the maintenance of its population. I understand that Turtle Creek near Riverview is still a good place to view these fellows in their natural environment.

Nova Scotia has all the turtle kinds mentioned, and in addition has a relict population of *Blandings turtles* in the southwestern part of the province.

Nova Scotia has *garter snakes*, as we do, and the strikingly beautiful *ribbon snake* as well, which New Brunswick does not. The ribbon snake looks like a glamorous garter snake to which it is related. We have in common a few smaller snake species: *red-bellied*, *green* and *ring-necked*.

Fish:

I never cease to be amazed at the number of fish in the sea and in the larger bodies of inter-connected freshwater. Over 100 species of fishes have been recorded in the marine environment, and there are over 25 species that are strictly freshwater. A number in the freshwater are deliberate introductions. Some of these successful "plants" are the *small-mouthed black bass*, *chain pickerel*, *rainbow trout*, and *muskellunge*. Several kinds are confirmed anadromous (i.e., inhabitants of salt water, yet spawn in freshwater): *salmon*, *sea trout*, *sea sturgeon*, *striped bass*, *smelt*, *blue-back herring*, *gaspereau* and *shad* are the main ones. The *green eel* is our only fish that does the reverse; it lives most of its life in freshwater and spawns in the sea.

The largest fish in our inland waters is the *sea sturgeon*. They can go several hundred pounds, dwarfing the biggest *striped bass* or *salmon*, which optimistically might weigh in the 30 lb. range. We have to go to the marine environment to find the largest fish in our region, the *basking shark*, a slow-moving and docile plankton eater that can grow to 40 feet in length, almost as long as the larger *whales*.

At maturity the *redbelly dace* is about three inches long. It's at home in fresh water and is about as small as any of our native fish species, although the *sticklebacks*, that live in both brackish and marine waters, aren't much bigger.

Pipefish, which look like attenuated seahorses to which they are related, are found in both inshore and brackish waters. Some fish, strange in appearance, give a hint of their appearance by their names: *wrymouths*, *alligatorfish*, *lumpfish*, *eelpout* and *butterfish*.

We have nearly 400 species of birds that have been recorded within the land mass of New Brunswick, or in the coastal waters of the province. A recent addition in the fall of 2002 was a relative of the falcon from far to the south: a crested *caracara*. An individual of that species spent some time on the Acadian Peninsula. This bird was classified as a vagrant, or a wanderer.

Very few species have of late been colonizers here. Only two recent candidates: the *oyster catcher*, which is suspected of nesting on one of the islands off Grand Manan, and the *bob white*, a quail which has self sustaining populations in southern Maine. The latter needs a boost from human hands in New Brunswick, surviving here only during very mild winters. The *loggerhead shrike*, which was once a rare breeder, seems to have left us as a nester for good.

Even in southern Quebec and southern Ontario their range is shrinking.

Two really large families, the waterfowl at 40 species, plus or minus one or two, and the wood warblers, at 36, together represent about 20% of our bird species.

We have over 40 species comprising *sparrows*, *finches*, and *grosbeaks*.

We have 9 *woodpeckers*, including the somewhat unusual *sapsucker*.

Including *vultures* and *owls*, we have 48 raptors, some of which are quite rare. For example, the *great grey owl* has been solidly documented only once, and only very keen birders have the king of the birds of prey, the *golden eagle* on their tally.

The gull-tern family and the sandpiper and allies each have about 30 species in their respective groups.

Having visited Europe, I feel we're a bit cheated in not having the mischievous *magpie*, even though it's found elsewhere in North America. A better range of "robin like" *thrushes* would be nice. The European *song thrush*, *fieldfare*, *redwing* and *ouzel* are all delightful birds. We're a bit light on native *doves* and *pigeons*, and it's not hard to envy other parts of North America in their variety of *hummingbirds*! We regularly only have the *ruby-throat*, whereas western North America has seven! And who couldn't fall for the delightful water-loving *dipper*, native to both Europe and the Pacific coasts of North America. It's related to the thrushes and actually walks on the bottom of streams foraging for insects.

A dozen marine mammals, and four times that number of land mammals, approximately, make up our furry fauna. The smallest is the aptly named *pygmy shrew*, weighed in grams, and the largest the *finback whale* assessed in tonnes. We're fortunate to have a part in the hoped for survival of the *North Atlantic right whale*, which has chosen our waters in which to spend the summer. Up to 20% of the total world population of these whales, about 350, might at any one time be in the outer Bay of Fundy.

 Speaking of big, we have a strong population of the world's largest deer, viz., the *moose*. Donor animals have gone to such places as Newfoundland, where introduction has been very successful.

We apparently never did have native *wapiti* or *elk*, and no *bison* ever did penetrate the dense forests of New Brunswick.

Less than a century ago, we had significant numbers of *caribou*. Alas, our particular variety has been extirpated.

Two of our common mammals, the *porcupine* and the *raccoon*, would seem happier and more in place further south. And, while there are no confirmed records yet, it seems likely that our first marsupial, the  *opossum*, the only pouched mammal north of Mexico, is steadily coming closer with each mild winter. Also, our native *snowshoe hare* may have to share some ground with the *cottontail rabbit* in years to come. These true rabbits are as close as southern Maine.

No one had to help the *coyote* to become established here, sort of avenging what we did to his big relative the *wolf*. There are no *gophers* in New Brunswick, and our only *ground squirrel* is the ambling *ground hog* or *woodchuck*. We're well supplied with native *mice* and small rodents; among the most delightful are the two kinds of jumping mice and the beautiful deer mice. The last mentioned has been implicated as an occasional carrier of the deadly (to humans) hanta virus.

Friends in the U.K. rhyme off a great number of native bats that most New Brunswickers have never heard of. The message for us seems to be that with our relatively sparse population of "flying mice" we should put more weight on conservation, leaving them be in the over-wintering caves and in breeding colonies where they're doing no real harm, and finally putting up bat houses specifically for them. Isn't that what good stewardship is all about?

3. A Morning Chorus to Introduce the Day and the Play

The spring and early summer dawn chorus of birds, and the other sounds of nature are doubly welcome after the long, nearly forever winter. Pre-dawn sees creatures of the night scurrying home. The soft-eyed, *white-tailed doe* moves deeper into shadow. A female *raccoon* hurries along, her mischievous young hopefully still curled up in the hollow tree where they live. Overhead a male *barred owl* calls out his trademark: "who cooks for you........who cooks for you alllllllllllll?" In a swamp pool *spring peepers* and *green frogs*, that have filled the dark with their strident calls and chug-a-rums, fall silent with the growing light. A foraging *mink* makes no discernible sound as he closes in on a *green frog*.

A Walk Into Spring

Rewinding back to the 1940s, it's the third week in May, and Jim Edwards, a well respected resident of *White Head* on the *Kingston Peninsula*, has been running his sawmill flat out for a month now. It's a warm morning, there's only a slight breeze, the air is loaded with the smell of billberry and apple blossoms.

Jim surprises his crew. Jack is occupied filing the headsaw, and someone else is adjusting the carriage; a third is re-stocking a peavey, when Jim exclaims, "Let's go, boys. We'll take a short walk to welcome spring!"

Enthusiastic, like kids out of school, the crew head up a road through a field, following a full, rushing brook coming from woods on the hill behind the sawmill. George brings his fishing rod.

The first *bobolinks* are flitting in the new green emerging from the dry brown grass of the past season. The males with their quiltwork backs of buff and brown patches position themselves to display to the monochrome brown females as they sing their sparkling "Bob-o-link, bob-o-link, spink spank spink!"

From overhead the barely musical notes of passing *grackles* assault the ears.

From a well branched *spruce*, there comes a prolonged chipping serenade. It's the trim, gray-breasted, chestnut-capped *chipping sparrow*. If he attracts a mate, their tidy nest might just be in the same *spruce*. It will be lined with horse hair if that is available; in lieu of this, some other animal's hair. Suddenly, from a newly-leaved *alder* comes a "witchety, witchety" call. The small olive-green warbler with a black face mask turns out to be a *northern yellowthroat*.

In a large *willow*, a flock of eye-catching *yellow and black warblers* are chasing after flies and other insects. They have flown a long way from their wintering grounds, and they're very hungry.

The most eye-catching of the birds is the *yellow warbler*. It pauses for a few seconds, throwing back its head, singing clearly, "Sweet, sweet, I'm so sweet!" A different ending and the song is characteristic of many warbler songs.

Along the edge of a nearby pool of water, the yellow *palm warbler* is gleaning breakfast. This bird isn't singing but is noticeably wagging its tail, its trademark.

From a nearby *crabapple* branch a *song sparrow* pours forth a pleasing liquid melody. Its scientific name describes it as the sparrow with the melodious song. One might wonder if, in our own dim past, bird song such as this brought caveman to the realization that we too could make pleasant song, if only a whistled imitation.

The road to the woods now crosses the brook by a sturdy log bridge. George baits his hook and drops his line. Instantly a *brook trout* strikes, but wriggles free. It was only a little one! George will try again at the *beaver* pond further upstream.

In the near distance the strong, clear, high-pitched notes of the *white-throated sparrow* sound. Some in our country say the white-throat sings "Sweet Canada, Canada, Canada" or "I love Canada, Canada, Canada." Others, along with our friends and neighbours in New England, claim it's saying, "Old Sam (or Tom) Peabody, Peabody, Peabody."

Among the leaves at the base of some *beeches* and *birches* by the water, the warbler that looks like a sparrow is kicking through forest litter. Its orange cap identifies it as an *ovenbird*. Its mate nearby gives the characteristic call, a loud "Teacher, teacher, teacher."

The mill workers saunter past a vigorous group of young *fir*s, a bit bigger than your average Christmas tree. Several warblers with fine, needle-like bills are paying attention to thick, dark-green foliage. Maybe they're after newly emerged *budworms*?

A *magnolia warbler* calls "Weeta, weeta, weeteo." With his striking yellow and black striped breast he contrasts nicely with a *yellow-rump warbler*, who has an inverted black horseshoe on his white breast. The yellow-rump, slightly bigger than the magnolia, has a pleasant but weak warbling song.

From a tall *hemlock* a bird with a neon-orange breast

trills after delivering some longer notes. It has an interesting name; it's the *blackburnian warbler*. Perhaps it was bird song such as his that inspired Thoreau when he wrote "The birds I heard (today) sung as freshly as if it had been the first morning of creation." Walking by some hardwoods, the little party spots a striped black and white bird working the trunk of a white birch. First they think it's a *chickadee*. It's actually the *black and white warbler*. Its long song is a bit painful to the ear; it's pitched very high and sounds like metal on metal without the benefit of lubrication!

Then from a low sapling a striking warbler, whose name describes its appearance, gives forth a slow refrain which is interpreted as "I am.... so.... la... zee". It's the (somewhat rare in New Brunswick) *black-throated blue warbler*, which is mint, and beautiful.

Further along, a dreamy, lisping zee, zee, zo, zee comes wafting down from a large *cedar*. It's a moment before the singer shows himself. First to appear from pale green foliage is a yellow head, then a prominent black throat; the back appears, drab olive-green. It's the *black-throated green warbler*.

The mill workers' goal is a conveniently placed bench beside a *beaver* pond. While the others rest, George proves that he's a fisherman. Casting his fly out onto the insect-dimpled surface, he hooks one pan-sized *trout* after another, up to half a dozen. Quickly he rolls them in cool, damp, *sphagnum moss* and places them in his creel. They'll go into the frying pan back at the mill.

The others are too busy watching their fisherman friend to see a *bittern* skulking away, but the sinuous wake of a departing *muskrat* catches their attention. The *Aspen* and *birch* that used to grow around the pond have been mostly cut down, and the *beaver* colony has apparently moved downstream. Meanwhile *tree swallows*, with their iridescent blue backs catching the sun, skim back and forth over the water, diminishing the insect population. An *olive-sided flycatcher* takes up a station on a dead stub of a tree and calls out "Quick, three beers," between sallies out for flies. In the distance in the valley of the stream a *belted kingfisher* calls loudly. They hear him several seconds before he comes barreling into view.

George wants to try fishing near the old *beaver* lodge, then from the top of this five-meter-wide pile of sticks. The elevated platform to cast from is a good choice. A one-pounder with the square tail of a mature trout is his first prize.

In the tangle surrounding an inlet brook, a perky little song prefaced by a distinct chip sounds forth. Then the songster creeps into view. It has a warm yellow breast, and a black necklace which identifies it as a *Canada warbler*. Its beautiful, lilting song has elements similar to the louder sound that the tiny *winter wren* produces in approximately 7 seconds.

A small bird runs along the water's edge, grabbing insect prey from the surface. Its tail-bobbing habit confirms it as the *northern waterthrush*, a member of the numerous warbler clan.

The return to the mill is also eventful. As they leave

the pond behind, the men hear the drumming of the *ruffed grouse* coming from a ridge half a mile away. Among the young newly-leaved *maples* and *birches* some brightly coloured, yellow and red and black warblers are flitting about, spreading their wings and fanning their tails. They are a small flock of *redstarts*, which not only glean but catch flies between the branches in short flights. The males are the ones with the red. At intervals, the male gives forth a thin, high-pitched song with a distinctive downslurred ending. A tidy nest could be placed close to the trunk 15 to 20 feet above the ground. The nest is camouflaged by bits of birch bark.

About halfway down the hill, one of the party points out a robin-sized bird with a striking red-triangle on its breast. All hands agree it's a beauty. Its singing is like a slower version of the robin's song. It's the *rose-breasted grosbeak*. Suddenly a *hummingbird* zips by so fast it's a blur. It's almost confused with a large bumblebee! From a stage provided by a stump, a *dark-eyed junco* male, stylish in his contrasting slate and white attire, gives a territorial ringing trill. Overhead, after launching himself from a *maple* branch the male *purple finch* gives an in-air pleasing soft warble. His modestly plumed mate, in brown and beige stripes, perches a little distance away.

Near the field and within sight of the mill, a soft song ending with a distinctive zip announces the blue, orange and yellow *parula warbler*. It's working from branch to branch in a tall *white ash*. Out in the field the *bobolinks* are still active, and suddenly Jim calls out, "Look over to the top rail of the snake fence." It's a pair of *bluebirds*. "I'll put a box together for them after lunch," Jim says. And then adds as an afterthought, "They're suffering a bit of a housing shortage."

While the men lunch on fried *trout* and eggs on the picnic table in the mill yard, their talk is punctuated by the tapping of a *hairy woodpecker*. A *robin* breaks into song – "Cheerily, cheer up, cheerio," from the top of a pile of fresh sawn lumber. *Barn swallows*, which are nesting in the loft above the mill, are darting about doing their best to cut down on the insect kingdom. A *red-winged blackbird* mistakenly takes the mill pond for a *cattail* marsh, pausing to utter his "conk-aree" while flaring the epaulets on the bend of his wings. After a few phrases he flies off looking for more suitable digs. As if giving approval a *blue jay* comes storming in: "Jay, Jay!"

The jay he sings a scanty lay,
As boy who would a fiddle play,
Strikes one bar from tuneful harp,
Then screeches into discord sharp.
                              Eben Pearson Dorr

4. Trees make the Scenery

Trees and forests define New Brunswick. Forest tracts and woodlots make the New Brunswick we know and love. Other than rock outcrops and fresh marshes, all the ground that makes up our Province is potentially forest. If it wasn't for our large expanses of unbroken forest, it's doubtful that we'd have such wildlife as *moose, pine marten*, the *pileated woodpecker* and the *great horned owl* in any meaningful numbers.

Tree communities cover the hills and rills like a cloak, protecting the landscape and making a perfect backdrop for the drama that may transpire. We tend to think of trees as individuals. Yet if trees could think they'd consider themselves part of a community of other trees, shrubs, and flowering plants, with associated mammals and birds, insects and spiders.

 Single species stands such as *jack pine* do occur, but they are rare. A common combination over much of this province is a trio consisting of two evergreens and a hardwood: *red spruce, balsam fir* and *white birch*. Multi-species stands, in which each of the members brings different advantages to the community, have greater resistance to insect attacks, problems with pathogens, and physical factors such as wind.

Some other communities that you might know and recognize can be completely deciduous, as in *sugar maple, beech* and *yellow birch* stands, or have an equal representation of both deciduous and evergreen, as *white pine* and *red oak*. Some pioneer stands come about from disturbances caused by man: for example, *white spruce* colonizing old fields. The "*cat spruce*," so-called because of its feline odour, often has an understory of alder. This is beneficial as the alder has the ability to fix nitrogen, thereby enhancing soil fertility. Over a long period of 20 years or better, the alders become decadent and "tired;" the spruce go on for another 40, but their fate is sealed too, as gradually shade-tolerant *red spruce* moves in, closely followed by *balsam fir*, and then *white birch*, and/or *red maple*. *White spruce*, not being a dedicated forest tree, will not persist.

When *red spruce* and *balsam* are harvested, *white birch* outdistances its two partners in the regeneration phase, acting as nurse and trainer. The hardwood leaves, which are all dropped annually, increase soil fertility, returning much more to the soil than the conifers do, which don't get rid of all their leaves (needles) in one season. (The rate of leaf drop in these conifers is about every 4 to 11 years for each individual needle's replacement.)

White pine, our tallest tree, is the monarch of the evergreens. 150 years ago the king's representative used to inscribe the bark of these trees with a broad arrow, reserving them for the crown. Back then many specimens towered over 100 feet in height. They were slated for masts for the Royal Navy.

Queen of the broad-leaved trees is the *American elm.* Its maximum height at 115-120 feet (35 meters) makes it a very imposing tree, especially with its wide vase-shaped crown and often open-growing habit. Elms occur naturally on the floodplains and intervale lands. Our Loyalist forebears, barely surviving the winter of 1783-1784 at St. Anne's Point (now part of Fredericton), were encouraged to eat the elm leaves of early spring by knowledgeable native neighbours. This, and no doubt other acts of kindness, probably guaranteed their survival to the summer.

The temptation to enjoy the shade of the great *elms* is really unwise, considering that branches may come crashing down without notice, leading to the Old English saying: "The Ellum hateth man and waiteth!" Sadly, like a few other of our native trees, this stately tree, once widely planted along the streets of Fredericton and other towns, has been afflicted by a malady. In the case of the elm it's the insidious *Dutch elm disease*, communicated from tree to tree very effectively by a tiny beetle. The elm's difficulties are not good for the orange and black *northern oriole*, which favours the tips of the pendant branches as a secure anchor for its sac-like nest, and the *bald eagle*, which is attracted to the central crown of the *elm* to place its one-tonne cradle. Dead *elms* are a temporary boon to the *pileated woodpecker*. The pileated usually only uses its carved out home for one season, releasing it to a secondary-cavity nester like the *wood duck*, the *common goldeneye* (affectionately called the "whistler"), and the sleek *hooded merganser*.

Basswood (called linden or lime in Europe), the *butternut* (white walnut), and the *bur white oak* are a trio of trees that we are fortunate to have in New Brunswick, as they reach their most eastern limit here.

The *white oak* is the most restricted, found naturally only around the shores of Grand Lake.

There's a theory that the *butternut*, with its edible nuts, was deliberately introduced by early native people living in the St. John River valley. This tree is found in the eastern townships of Quebec; then there's a break until you reach the upper Saint John, from where it's found to Tidewater 400 hundred miles away. It is known that the First Nations people were first to discover that a bright yellow dye could be extracted from the fruit husks.

Basswood, rare east of the St. John River valley, is quite regularly encountered along the river's banks, and on islands in the channel of the Saint Croix River. There is, however, an extremely large single tree at the head of Rayworth's Beach at the southern end of Long Island in the Kennebecasis.

According to Norse mythology, the first man was plucked from the trunk of a mighty *ash*. They apparently saw the human form in the sparse strong branches of this tree. Of *ashes*, we have three kinds: *white, red* and *black*. All are the firewood procurer's joy, as they can be kindled upon cutting and leave nothing after combustion but ash.

Black ash particularly was sought out by Native basket weavers, and under an old agreement this tree was reserved for their use. All ashes prosper where the ground is wet. Red and black grow best in the freshet zone. The *red ash* is often an associate of the *silver maple*, or the *red maple*. *White ash*, the most likely to become a large forest tree, will pioneer open hillsides, especially if the soil is well-supplied with moisture.

Red maple, so-named for its contribution of red foliage to the fall parade of colour, also has striking red flowers showing in the latter days of April. *Red maples* don't all dwell in the low ground; some keep company on rocky slopes with our largest maple, the *sugar*.

The orange glow of the autumn *sugar maple* is not the colour of the silhouette of this five-pointed leaf on our national flag; that red is the red of the red maple. This is the tree that's garnered fame and infamy due to being a source of the high market value "bird's eye" lumber.

Two smaller maples live as understory trees in the hardwood or mixed wood stands. The larger, big enough to make firewood, is the *striped maple* (sometimes called "moose wood" as that big deer in hard winters will strip the bark). *Mountain maple* has a leaf similar to the red maple, but is only a large shrub. White-tails munch on this one.

The birch and spruce tree families have three members each. Representing the birches we have white, yellow and gray. For the spruces we have white, red, and black.

The white birch is the most widespread of the family. It is the preferred tree to provide bark for canoes, once so important to the travel of native peoples. Why is the bark of this tree so dazzlingly white? One theory is that *white birch*, a persistent fire follower, developed a covering that would reflect heat from blackened ground after an intense forest fire. Slower growing trees, like the spruce and fir, owe the white birch for protection, as it acts as a nurse for the seedlings of the slower-growing evergreens. For this reason, and for its overall eye-catching beauty, it has earned the title "lady of the forest." Our two black and white patterned woodpeckers, the robin-sized *hairy* and the smaller *downy* seem well camouflaged when on a white birch. The *downy woodpecker* concentrates on the smaller branches while the *hairy* works the trunks.

Yellow birch not only grows to a larger size than the white birch, it has a life span of over a hundred years. A *white birch* is old at 70. Don't be fooled by the changes in the bark texture of the yellow birch at various stages in its life. Young vigorous trees have yellowish curly bark. On ancient trees, the covering becomes furrowed and forms great plates. Yellow birch can be made into good lumber, and is good firewood. It has about twice the heat value of white birch, which itself burns very well.

The *gray* or *wire birch* is a small, crooked tree, often restricted to improvised soils. Its typical associates are *jack pine*, and *aspen*. Acadians have this saying about the effort required to manufacture this tree into firewood: "It has to be limbed three times: once when you fell it; again when you transport it; and finally when you put it in the woodbox!" The message: it's limby. Anyway it's great for placing small nests if you're a white-throated sparrow, or a Swainson thrush.

Red spruce, growing in thick, tall stands that shade out undergrowth, is the ideal lumber tree of New Brunswick. It could well be our Provincial Tree, but our friends in Nova Scotia beat us out! Our New Brunswick Provincial Tree is the beautifully symmetrical balsam fir.

Many fine stands of red spruce grow along the Fundy shore, with old growth persisting and protected by living in the steep valleys of the Big and Little Salmon Rivers. As lumber, it's marketed under the grade "northern species." As a natural Christmas tree, either completely wild or sheared as it develops, it has no peer.

The *black spruce* is the quite slim cosmopolitan sister of the *red spruce*. The *red* is restricted to the east; the *black* lives and prospers from Alaska to Cape Spear, Newfoundland. This is a tough tree; it occurs in bogs, on rocky hillsides, and out into the muskeg of the north. Its persistent cones don't give up their seeds easily. The crowns, with cones set above the growing portion, can be scorched but not burned if a wildfire rushes through. Then they lose their seeds. When the coals cool, the seeds flutter down to a bare seed bed. They are ready to germinate with the first rain shower. Communities of *spruces* are home to the *moose* and *gray jay*.

The white spruce is not really a deep forest tree. It is a pioneer of exposed places, as in old fields, or open strips of coast.

Aspens and poplars are rapid growing and prolific. The *trembling* or *quaking aspen*, so called because the leaves flutter noisily in the slightest breeze, is the most widespread. Its preferred habitat is along streams and lakes. It's the preferred food of the beaver.

The balsam poplar doesn't attract much attention from the beaver. It has a strong odour emanating from the new buds in spring, giving credence to the Biblical sounding name *Balm of Gilead*.

The biggest is the forest growing large-toothed aspen, the name referring to the deep indentations on the leaves.

The beech, its paper thin leaves turning rich orange in the fall, does its part in adding to the fall colour show. When beech nuts are plentiful, wildlife has a feast; the little *deer mouse*, the *white-tailed deer* and the *bear* zero in on the bounty. *Chipmunks* and both *red* and *gray squirrels* store the three-corned husks, stripping the covering later to reach the high energy white meat. *Ruffed grouse* and *blue jays* are among the birds that are attracted to the bounty.

Some of the finest *hemlocks* in New Brunswick are preserved and protected in Fredericton's Odell Park. It's estimated that some of these trees are over 400 years old, and they're massive. *Hemlock* were once felled and left to moulder; only the bark, useful for tanning, was removed. It's one of the paradoxes of nature that this evergreen that can become so large has very small, hazelnut-sized cones. The crown of the *hemlock* is a favoured feeding site of the *golden-crowned kinglet*, and in summer a home for *blackburnian* and other wood *warblers*.

White pine, due to the texture of the wood, is a "soft" pine, easy to work. The other two native *pines*, the *jack* (already discussed) and the *red*, are "hard" pines.

Red pine, with its long, dark green needles and flaky red bark, is a beautiful tree, symmetrical and full crowned. *Red pine* shares a survival trait with *red oak*, in that they both have a tap root, enabling them to withstand serious windstorms. Red pine is an extremely uniform species, and its form is consistently predictable. This desirable attribute can be related to a very restricted range in the southern Appalachians during the last ice age. The red pine was caught in a "genetic bottleneck," where all or most of the trees of the donor population had superior features. One of the most beautiful natural stands in the province is of fire origin and located at the head of the First Nepisiquit Lake in Mount Carleton Provincial Park.

Northern white cedar, of which I could sing praises for a long time, provides excellent, light, strong, and rot resistant lumber for decks and lawn furniture. For the Loyalist and Irish pioneers it was a source of rail fences, which if built in the snake or zig zag fashion, could be economically done without any hardware. First Nations peoples knew of *cedar wood's* good qualities, using it for the frames of their birch bark canoes. Even the outer bark woven into mats was useful around the wigwam. During the depths of winter, *deer* do best if their yard includes a *cedar grove*. Cedar foliage is many times more nutritious than the alternative, fir. And what's a *cedar waxwing* without a cedar?

The *hop-hornbeam* is a small broad-leaved tree that gets its name from the appearance of its fruit sacs, which look like the hops used in brewing. An alternate name is *ironwood*, referring to the strength and toughness of the wood. Pioneers, ever resourceful, used it for wagon axles and wheel hubs.

Finally, larch. Depending on what part of the province you're from, this tree has some picturesque local names: tamarack and hackmatack are two. It is a deciduous conifer which turns a smoky orange in November just before shedding its needles. It then earns the honour of being "the last light in the forest." The wood is excellent for heating the house; reputedly it can warp a stove top, it burns so hot. The lumber is grainy but strong. Many birds like living around *larch* trees, including the *spruce grouse*, which ingests the long soft needles.

5. Bushy Little Guys

The smaller trees keep the understory together. They are no less important than their bigger brothers and sisters. In the total kinds present, shrubs and bushes outnumber trees about 2 to 1 in New Brunswick.

In the small tree group we have two kinds of *alder*, two *maples*, three *mountain ashes*, a couple of *cherries*, two *elders*, a *dogwood* or two, and finally a whole array of *shadbushes/billberries*. For convenience and efficiency we'll call this last group by their proper scientific name: the <u>Amelanchiers</u>.

It's mind-boggling to sort out the *shrubs*, especially what we tend to call simply *bushes*. For the province it is possible to find nine members of the *blueberry* family, and a dozen *wild roses*, at least 14 *hawthornes*, about two dozen different *willows*. The willows are difficult to sort out; several kinds are simply labeled *pussy willows*. Then *hazelnut*, and *witch hazel*, *daphne*, *barberry*, and *bittersweet*. *Daphne*, *barberry* and a number of the *roses* are generally garden escapees. *Lilac* is persistent where it grows, but doesn't spread.

Trees generally produce seeds that have no fleshy covering. Many *bushes* produce *berries*, often bird-attracting red, purple or sometimes blue, or other colours. Many are high energy and sought after, and maybe even vital at certain seasons for the survival of many *birds*.

What shrubs lack in size they make up for in character. They seem to cover the spectrum of deciduous and evergreen, alternate or opposite leaf arrangements, and a great variety of flower patterns and colours.

Gale grows along beaches and as a border to banks of stagnant creeks. It shares beach habitat, especially along the Kennebecasis, with a *potentilla* with attractive yellow blossoms. Gale often keeps company with *leatherleaf* or *chamaedaphne*. The observant will note that individual gale plants will have a profusion of pale yellow or slightly magenta blossoms in early spring. The female plant is the most richly coloured.

Leatherleaf clumps are sought out for nesting by the female *ring-necked duck*.

Sweet fern (*spirea*) that's prevalent under *jack pine* in eastern King's and much of Westmorland, Kent, and Northumberland is neither a "fern" nor "sweet!" Farmers don't love spirea, calling it hardhack for good reason. It seems even to defy a land-breaking plough. This attitude doesn't dissuade the *yellow warbler*, as this gorgeous warbler does love spirea! Even if many other shrubs are present in a weedy meadow or intervale, 90% plus of the neat, down-lined nests will be in spirea, a location which doesn't keep them from being parasitized by the *cowbird*.

Twin for the white flowered "spirea" (hardhack) is the mauve flowered *meadow sweet*. It likes wet, non-agricultural land, and isn't very aggressive.

A native holly (*winterberry*) often retains its bright red berries till Christmastide. It doesn't have prickly leaves like the commercial variety; in fact it's bare of leaves early in the fall.

An attractive evergreen shrub, the *Canada yew*, is sought out by *moose*, as deer seek out cedar. Like the foliage of cedar, yew is rich in vitamin C. Not prolific or fast growing, this shrub (also called ground hemlock) may have other consumers besides moose, as it's targeted as an ingredient for cancer cures. In growth pattern it bears a superficial resemblance to ground juniper, which further south has small tree relatives. Before synthetics, the powdery blue berries were used as a flavour for gin. They can be safely consumed fresh, though they're a bit gummy and sharp – most samplers won't eat enough to spoil dinner! It favours shade and moist, rich soils.

One shrub seems to bloom out of phase, flowering in the late fall. It's the *witch hazel* that has adapted to flower in southern New Brunswick as late as early November. Unique, the flower petals are yellow and strap-like, and are quite visible, as at blooming time the leaves have normally fallen. The next stage are nut-like capsules that release the two tiny seeds like a touch-me-not, or noisily. This happens the following year. Most of us are aware of the medicinal properties of witch hazel, but did you know that a Y-shaped branch can be pressed into service as a water seeking divining rod?

I've seen witch hazel growing along the high water mark along the Kennebecasis and the St. John. Stephen Clayden, Curator of Botany at the New Brunswick Museum, tells me that the Mount Douglas trail out of Welsford is a good place to enjoy a good number of these interesting shrubs. Look for a sprawling shrub somewhat reminiscent of the unrelated hazelnut.

The *beaked hazelnut*, usually just called hazelnut, produces nuts good for human consumption that are identical to the commercially available filberts except that they are a bit smaller. Personally, I think these wild ones are sweeter! The fraternity of *deer mice*, *chipmunks* and both *red* and *gray squirrels* seem to know where every nut-laden bush is, because I challenge anyone to arrive there first.

One pleasure that won't be denied the "bumbling human" is the enjoyment of the floral display in the spring.

As you come onto a hazel bush, the first things you'll note are the pendant, creamy yellow male catkins. While examining these look to the tips of the branches. Here are the magenta tufts which are the female flowers. This site is the future location of the nuts, often occurring in pairs.

Hazel bushes don't aggressively grow in the open, favouring field edges, fence rows, and under the canopy of open hardwood stands. Both *deer* and the *ruffed grouse* like the buds and the nuts. *Blue jays* take the nuts and hide them.

The *alternate leaf dogwood* is a scattered and rare tree in the southern part of the province. Its white-berried relative, the *red osier*, generally a prostrate shrub, is abundant around streams and seasonally flooded islands. Whimsical children at play term the fruit "poison berries." They're bland, but not poisonous! Birds tend to ignore them, but *deer, moose*, even pastured *cattle* eat the red stems. Probably good crude fiber.

Its branching habit of branches coming off the main stem at right angles gives the crown a distinctive urn shape. As is true of all dogwoods including the partridge or bunchberry the leaves have prominent arch venation which is distinctive. Many insects are attracted to the stems and leaves of this small tree. The plus side is warblers and vireos secure dinner courtesy of the dogwood! The deep blue-purple berries ripen in late summer, food for robins, thrushes, grouse, deer and even the black bear.

Sometimes the unrelated *hobblebush*, one of our three native <u>Viburnums</u>, is called dogwood, and is often gathered for forcing in April. The white (sterile) flowers are striking and make a nice early spring decorative in-house display. The fertile flowers, which are greenish and much more humble, surround the showy ones in a circle. The obvious flowers are targets for bees, hover flies and other pollinators.

Our other two viburnums are important to wildlife as food which persists through the fall and into winter. The misnamed high bush "cranberry" (V. trilobum) is notable for lasting fruit, sometimes available for the *robin*'s return in March. Translucent red, the conveniently clustered fruit is attractive to *grosbeaks* and *ruffed grouse*.

Another viburnum, the wild raisin, is so-called because the ripe fruit becomes wrinkled and deep blue-black in colour and resembles dried grapes, raisins. Not especially favoured by birds, I've seen *bears* strip them with gusto! The foliage of this shrub turns a distinctive pink in fall.

A fourth viburnum, the *nanny berry*, is restricted to Charlotte County.

A unique feature of most viburnums is the absence of bud scales, which permits the winter botany buff to see the form of the embryonic leaves as they'll unfold in the spring. It also indicates that the viburnums are reaching their northern limit in our area.

A few *heath plants* have eye-catching flowers: *rhodora*, *andromeda*, and *kalmia*. At least one has a reputation for having foliage that is medicinal: Labrador tea. From this group it's only the Vacciniums that produce a widely desirable fruit. *Deer* not only savour *blueberries* themselves, but will also gnaw the stems of bushes in winter if the snow doesn't hide them too deeply. *Ripe blueberries* please everything from *robins* to *bears*. Early returning *Canada geese* will wedge out *bog cranberries* from the lingering ice in the marshes. *Rock cranberries*, as do *blueberries*, feed both *ruffed* and *spruce grouse*.

We have two very similar kinds of *alders*. Here in Atlantic Canada, a put down is to refer to someone's family tree as an alder!

Most timber cruisers disdain alders, having had experience of trying to run a line through a bed of these confused tangles when the snow is deep and unsettled. But alders have a number of redeeming features. The roots harbour nitrogen fixing nodules which greatly improve the soil in old and often "worn-out" fields that the alders have invaded. The annual leaf fall also adds considerable nitrogen. And the tangle of alder roots slows soil erosion.

Wildlife benefits from the various features of alders; many a *white-tail fawn* has spent its early days bedded down in the protection of an alder thicket. *Hares* don't feed much on alder twigs or leaves but they do appreciate the cover. Ruffed grouse are often found in alder beds, eating the seeds or buds in winter, and in the summer they are great for brood rearing, as the leaf litter is populated with insects and spiders, a good source of protein for the developing chicks. The *woodcock* and the *alder* go together like hand and glove; damp areas between the alder clumps are great for probing for *earthworms*, the "timberdoddles'" favourite food! The thick cover serves the *woodcock* as it does the *grouse*, a secure home to raise the family. *Robins*, the *veery*, the *catbird*, the *swamp sparrow* and the *common yellowthroat* all like to nest among the alders.

Like their cousins the *birches*, *alders* often give a protected start to *white spruce* and *balsam fir*. If you study the structure of an established alder clump, note that it's often open to the sky in the centre. This is where a young conifer will attempt a start, its seed easily gaining a foothold in the loosened soil.

Alder stands are old at 20-30, and begin to break up. In the meantime the young spruce/fir has reached the top of the alder bed canopy. It then begins to shade its protector. Alders can't tolerate anything but full sun, so they gradually die out.

Two kinds of *alder*, the stream side "*speckled*" and the upland "*mountain*" *alder*, complement each other by dividing up the landscape so that there's always an alder ready to go. To insure that the two species aren't likely to exchange pollen, their catkins flower roughly three weeks apart, with the somewhat hardier and more northern speckled going first. The speckled alder catkins, along with *pussy willows*, are often the first source of pollen and nectar for early foraging bees.

For those that would like a really hot fire, alder wood is tops; however it's time consuming to prepare, and possibly embarrassing if it is seen in storage by neighbours or other visitors! Alder wood, as well, is a raw material for charcoal.

The *elder* family is represented by two members in

New Brunswick. Like in the alder twins, mistaken and inefficient pollination is inhibited by spacing flowering. Again, as with the alder pair, the *red-berried elder* flowers in very early May, but the *elderberry* delays blooming until well into July. At any season the two can be separated by checking the pith of the easily broken twigs. Conveniently, the "red-berried" has reddish-cinnamon pith. The elderberry has white. Both elders are reliable producers of fruit. *Robins*, *thrushes* and *catbirds* consume the fruit in quantity, with the flycatching *phoebe* and *kingbird* being occasional feeders. The soft twigs are often browsed in winter by *snowshoe hares*, *deer* and *moose*.

Apparently because the seed cluster is velvety the widely occurring *sumac* has the modifier "*staghorn.*" To the human eye the hairy red berries may not look like attractive food, yet virtually every native perching bird utilizes them for food. *Ruffed grouse* is also partial to them, the seeds being so hard that they serve for a time at least as a grinding agent in the gizzard. As anyone, like my good spouse for instance, that has tried to nurture this shrub in "deer country," will tell you in Caps, *deer* crave the twigs.

We have three *mountain ashes* that grow profusely in southern New Brunswick. The two natives are augmented by the well naturalized European species. To the casual observer they are pretty much inseparable. Actually, they are misnamed and not even close to the true ash tree in relationship. They are members of the huge "rose" family, and in tune with their true relatives the wild roses, cherries, amelanchiers, hawthorns, apples and peaches they are universally loved by many species of wildlife for food. This includes both mammals and birds, birds particularly.

As with other early, bitter-flavoured fruit, mountain ash improves in palatability as summer merges into fall and winter. *Robins*, especially, gorge on it, probably sensing that it is a source of both iron and vitamin C. Both *cedar* and *bohemian waxwings*, and the *evening* and *pine grosbeaks* also consume it. In cities, native birds may have to be quick to beat the hordes of *starlings* that strip many trees in a short time. In the quiet sections of the countryside *ruffed grouse* sample it, and fall fattening *bears* gobble fruit clusters, small twigs and leaves included.

Both *choke* and *pin cherry* fruit are eagerly eaten by many birds, including the *ruffed grouse* and a number of mammals. Some of the mammals would be expected: *mice* and *chipmunks*. Others would cause a rational person to scratch the head: *coyotes, red foxes, skunks* and *deer*. From the human perspective, attitudes haven't changed much over the years, and most would relate to the following comment by American colonist William Wood, who penned in 1634 these words: *"They so furre the mouth that the tongue will cleave the roofe, and the throat will wax hoarse with swallowing those red Bullies!"* Amen!
    Editor's Note: Yes, but wait till they turn black, just before they dry up. Good!

Guess I'm biased, but personally I'm a fan of the *Amelanchier*, a.k.a., *shadbush, juneberry, serviceberry*, and commonly in much of southern New Brunswick, *billberry*. It starts being generous and giving with that universal bountiful showing of flowers in early to mid-May. As these inflorescences appear before the leaves, they're enjoyed to the full, and early enough that winter weary folks really savour them. A tad seedy, the fruit is both sweet and bountiful. While a gourmet might not promote this fruit for pies, this writer can attest to its pleasant and distinct flavour when used in this way. Mammals that enjoy the berries are somewhat expected: *squirrels*, *chipmunks*, and *deer mice*. Not expected are *red foxes*, *coyotes*, *martens* and *fishers*. In winter the buds and twigs are food for *deer, hares, flying squirrels*, and *ruffed grouse*. It's no surprise that the *robin*, the *hermit thrush*, and *catbirds* eat the berries. But it's a bit surprising that *sapsuckers*, and *woodpeckers* of all ilks, and *blue jays* and *chickadees* even go for them. Our native peoples incorporated the similar berries of the *Saskatoon bush* in pemmican. Besides flowers and fruit, the leaves of this tree add a pleasing pink to the fall foliage parade.

To conclude this chapter the praises of *wild apples* and *crabapples* will be sung. Unlike many domesticated shrubs and other plants, the apple family self-seeds with little encouragement. No doubt it's often transported involuntarily by its dedicated consumers: *bears, raccoons, deer* and birds. *Robins* returning "too early" often receive their first food by eating the seeds out of winter-softened still-on-the-branch apples. Apple blossoms are a magnet for *bees, wasps*, and early *butterflies*, which in turn tow in *cedar waxwings, rose-breasted grosbeaks, scarlet tanagers, bluebirds* and *Baltimore orioles*. The first *hummingbirds* of the season are often seen around the crowns of flowering apple trees. Fall foraging *grouse* work in conjunction with *deer*, eating or picking at those on the ground. *Bears* seem to sense that a feed of apples, the tarter the better, will help purge their system before the long sojourn in the den. To assist wildlife, there's two things that can be done: prune, and stimulate by removing competition from any wild apple trees under your control, also plant tried, hardy types. Good

Luck!

By the way, any apple wood gained by maintenance won't be good for kindling. However, when it takes its place to continue a hot fire, the sweet fragrance from the burning wood is exquisite, especially if used in a fireplace.

6. True Beauty in the Wildflowers

In southern New Brunswick we have our best wildflower show just as soon as the snow melts. This is especially true of the flowers that grow in the woods. They're programmed to complete most of their development by the time the tree leaf canopy closes over them. Adaptation and evolution at play. It's all about survival.

One of the most attractive flowers is fortunately abundant: the yellow petalled *trout lily*. Where it grows profusely on favoured south-facing slopes, these areas take on a yellow glow. Most springs the earliest blooms can be found in the last few days of April, if a diligent search is made. Peak flowering is the first two weeks of May. This is the best time to take a leisurely stroll through the hardwoods, to enjoy this beautiful plant often in great swards. By mid May, other flowers, which are normally a bit later, will begin to show. Progress in flower development is so rapid that the observant will note advances with each day. If you're a camera freak, stock up on film. These flowers and their associates are super photogenic, yet due to breezes and their obedience to them, catching them on film can be challenging.

Trout lilies do best in damp soil under a hardwood stand. For neighbours they often have *red trillium, wild lily of the valley, spring beauty, toothwort* and maybe *Dutchman's breeches*. In support of the name, trout lily, for *Erythronium americanum*, the following is submitted: it flowers when the trout head upstream in the early spring, and the mottled leaves bear some resemblance to the flanks of our native *brook trout*. Also, it often grows on the banks of trout streams.

The *trout lily* shares a trait with other members of the Lily Clan. The bloom closes at night. When the flower opens the next morning under the warming rays of the sun, the opening is facing downwards. This is a practical adaptation. Rain isn't so apt to wash away the pollen, and non-flying insects that don't cross pollinate can't easily plunder it for food. The "plan" is to ship the pollen by *bee* or *wasp;* that is, by air, as far as is possible from the mother plant.

Trout lilies have a complex strategy for reproduction and establishment of the next generation. It's effective. Seeds resulting from the fertilized flowers in May ripen promptly by mid June, yet they won't germinate for a year, or until the next spring. The sprouting seed develops a corm, a bulb-like structure, at the surface. From the corms, threads called "droppers" emerge, and these plunge down into humus at about a 45 degree angle from the original seed. Out about 10 inches a new corm is produced. There are many of these, and each will produce its own leaf. The end result: lots of leaves and many fewer high quality flowers. All this growth activity has a benefit. The otherwise loose soils on slopes are bound by the roots, and erosion is slowed. It takes on average seven seasons to produce a trout lily from the original germinated seed. Something to bear in mind if the blooms are picked for a bouquet.

The white flowered *wild lily of the valley* has a smaller bloom than the *trout lily*. Peak flowering is into May, or about 10 days behind the trout lily. The flowers aren't the first thing that the woods-walker will note as he or she approaches a colony of these plants; it's the shiny dark green leaves. The success of a particular patch as far as flowering and eventual seed production goes is a delicate balance between light, moisture and nutrients. These plants have a delicate perfume; it's sharp yet sweet. You'll have to get close to pick it up. Eventually, in July, a translucent gray fruit comes along. When ripe later on, it will be ruby red. It will contain at least one seed. The flesh and the seed or seeds are food for the *white-throated sparrow*, *red squirrels*, *chipmunks* and *deer mice*. The *ruffed grouse* is about the largest animal that eats them.

In the neighbourhood of the lilies, clumps of *red trillium* may be present. Recall, *trillium* meaning all flower parts in threes, or multiples of three. Ten to a dozen plants may grow together. The flowers have an unpleasant odour of meat that's starting to go bad. Why? Early in the year flying pollinators are at a premium, and this trillium may have to rely on a wandering beetle. This unusual property of foul odour has stimulated a couple of folk names: "stinking Benjamin," and "wet dog trillium." The *painted trillium*, sporting pink veined petals, blooms a full fortnight after the red one, and doesn't have a bad odour. It doesn't have to! There are lots of flying pollinators by that time.

Dutchman's breeches, a close relative of the bleeding heart in your garden, actually has a somewhat saucy name. In colonial times breeches equated with buttocks! *Spring beauty* often grows in the same area. It has a white blossom. The *toothwort*, which favours wet depressions between the other spring flowers, has off-white flowers, and gets its name from the tooth-edged leaves. On the hardwood ridges of York and Carleton Counties, the saucy Dutchman is joined by *bloodroot* and *wild ginger*. Rare in New Brunswick is the *round-lobed hepatica*; it's restricted to the area of Currie Mountain, just north of Fredericton.

 As we get into June, the chalky white four-part flowers of the *bunchberry* appear. Not restricted to hardwoods, this plant grows well in mixed woods, or even in the shadow of evergreens. By late July the bright red berries are obvious, but not for long, as the same crowd that seeks out the fruit of *wild lily of the valley* relishes these too. Our bunchberry is part of the Cornus family, which includes one of our shrubs, the *red osier dogwood*, and a small tree, the *flowering dogwood* from further south. All members of this family have a unique venation pattern in the leaves. The veins form arches.

Moving away from the forest to a marsh edge or a wet meadow, some interesting flowers start appearing by early summer. The so-called *cuckoo flower* (a member of the mustard family) can turn the freshet edge white with it's blooms. It has earned this name as it can appear suddenly and unpredictably, like a cuckoo. A more appealing name is *lady's smock* as commemorated is this short poem;

Tread once again the stepping stones where
childhood feet had trod:
To stand among the lady's smock
and be a child of God.

The *purple avens*, alternately called "chocolate flower," has purplish petals. It keeps company with the *blue flag iris*. The exquisitely beautiful *Canada lily*, called *Turk's cap* further west, is a giant among native wildflowers. A healthy individual will have a dozen or more blooms per plant and be in the two meter height category. Around Grand Lake and Jemseg these plants flourish. The red *cardinal flower*, most eye-catching, grows out among the stones in the shallow water of streams in Charlotte and western York Counties. It's common along the St. Croix and Magaguadavic Rivers.

In the shallows of quiet water the white flowered *arrowhead* and the *plantain* are true aquatic plants. The *loosestrife* contingent is represented by some non-aggressive natives; the *swamp candle* is one, and the *yellow loosestrife* is the other. Clouding the issue is the entrance of the invasive *purple loosestrife*. Not behaving as it does in its native Europe, this robust plant is invading many types of wetland in our country, giving rise to the phrase; "purple plague." It hasn't attracted any efficient predators in eastern Canada, at least not yet.

Three damp-ground flowers that are attractive are *jewel weed*, *joe pye weed*, and *turtlehead*. *Jewel weed*, a *ruby-throated hummingbird* favourite is also known as *touch-me-not*. As hinted by the last name, this plant is a "toy of nature," as most small boys know, when the explosive seed cases are tapped just the right way. It's all about dispersal. *Joe pye weed* is named for a New England native medicine man. He claimed to have found a cure for rheumatism. *Turtlehead* with its cream-coloured blooms is a companion plant. Common in more extensive marshes, is the pink flowered *swamp milkweed*. Its larger relative, the dry land *common milkweed*, is vital to the prosperity of the monarch butterfly, as it's the preferred food of its black and green caterpillars.

Both *asters* and *goldenrods* have been lumped together as fall flowers. True of the former, but not of the latter. *Canada goldenrod* often shows flowers in July, which is hopefully not fall! Most asters are pale blue, for example the New England and the New York, both of which are common in N.B. Asters peak in mid-September after a few nearly frosty dawns. The flat-topped white aster is the largest native aster; it can go the height of the tallest basketball star. The whorled *wood aster* has pale mauve flowers, and it does grow in the open woods. Another aster that prefers clearings in the woods is the blue flowered *large-leaved aster*. (Basal leaves are up to eight inches wide, and are an aide to confirming the identity).

Late *goldenrod* could have a common name more in tune with its scientific name which is *Solidago gigantea*, as it can grow up to seven feet tall in preferred moist sites. It blooms through

September and into October defying mild frosts with impunity. Another sturdy goldenrod is the *seaside goldenrod* which has particularly rich yellow blooms. In total there's about 30 goldenrods in New Brunswick, and about half that number of asters. This amazing fall flower offering is joined by other families, for example the well named *pearly everlasting*, the *fall dandelion*, and the *black-eyed Susan*.

7. An Important Foundation

Non-flowering plants don't get a lot of press but are important nevertheless. *Ferns*, *mosses*, *clubmosses*, *lichens* and *algae* are important as a solid foundation.

We have a *fern* for all seasons, some two dozen in most parts of New Brunswick. There's a fern for all locations, even dessicated dry sites. The *three branched bracken* has these arid areas: upland pastures, untended *blueberry* fields, and dry rocky hillsides all to itself. Not a scourge here in our province, it's an invasive that's unwelcome in the sheep and cattle pastures of the U.K. Most of the other ferns like moisture, even if just dampness and shade. Three large ferns, going the height of a tall first grader by mid-summer, are the *cinnamon*, the *fiddlehead*, and the *interrupted*. The cinnamon is so-called because the club-like fertile leaves are covered with cinnamon fuzz. For many New Brunswickers, plucked fiddleheads are a special spring treat, boiled and served with either butter or vinegar. Our First Nation people started the tradition, regarding the unfurling fern, or "fiddlehead," as symbolic of the sun. It's the icon of the New Brunswick Craft Council. Due to their potential commercial value, cultivation of the fiddlehead has been tried, successfully. Fiddlehead ground is best if seasonally enriched by silt from the freshet.

The widely spaced leaflets on the prime stalks of the *royal fern* give it a distinct locust tree appearance. It likes its feet wet, often growing right in the bed of a running stream. It's a large fern like the fiddlehead. A fern living in the wet areas often bordering streams is the small *sensitive fern*. It has acquired the specific name due to its vulnerability to late frosts.

Colonizing huge areas on moist hillsides, and in open shady woods, is the lacy-leaved *hay-scented fern*. If you crush the leaflets between your hands, a smell somewhere between peaches and freshly cut grass will be released. More restricted than the hay-scented are several attractive woodland ferns; *long beech, oak* and the *New York fern*. *Polypody*, which has a peculiar leaflet arrangement of an alternating pattern, prefers to grow on huge boulders.

Related to ferns are the descriptively named *horsetails*. These low plants that appear on roadsides and waste ground early in the spring do look the part. *Clubmosses*, low attractive plants of the type you'd like to take home for you own landscaping plans are alternately called *ground pine.*

 *Lichens* (we have hundreds of kinds) are amazing plants. They are a unique "marriage" between an alga (this portion looks after photosynthesis) and a fungus (this portion handles water transport). Many kinds appear gray, brown or pale green, yet are all capable of manufacturing their own food with the help of the sun. Slow growing, they can't compete with aggressive flowering plants and must of necessity settle on dead tree limbs, tree bark, bare boulders, even shady buildings. Not many have common names; *lungwort* is one, and one of the *cladonias* has been misnamed "*reindeer moss.*" It's a favoured food of *caribou.*

 *Mosses* which are more like regular plants are also represented by many species, most of which again don't have common names. However, two large groups that do, in fact, have easy handles are the *feather mosses*, which grow under trees, and the bog and swamp-loving *sphagnums.* Sphagnums are able to hold 20x their weight in water and ecologically may assist their associate plants through the trial of a drought. Some others that did gain common names are the *hair-cap*, *broom*, *wavy undulatum*, *nodding pholia*, *shaggy moss* and the ribbed *bog moss.*

Two kinds of marine *algae*, *knotwrack*, and *bladderwrack*, are technically brown algas, quite similar in appearance, and do a thorough job covering nearly every boulder and ledge between Grand Manan and Cape Enrage. A protected and sheltered home among the wracks is sought out by *periwinkles, limpets* and *whelks*. Edible and healthful is a red alga, commonly known as *dulse*. The main harvest area in the world for this valuable plant is Dark Harbour, Grand Manan. Subtidal, and in sheltered, moderate current areas is the *devil's apron kelp*. It appears to be reminiscent of leather straps.

8. These Have Leading Roles

Not many life forms take what may be termed lead roles in the drama of nature. Those that do, unknowingly it seems, are the good Samaritans of the animal world. They provide direct and indirect benefits to other flora and fauna. Sometimes, because of the benefits they bestow, they are called keystone species. A few examples follow.

The beaver is one such species. Its "water works" provide both immediate and long range benefits to so many other kinds of wildlife that it would be difficult to list them all. Doing a bit of lumping, I'd say something like this: *aquatic plants* (especially *irises*), *arrowheads*, *yellow pond lilies*, *fragrant water lilies* and *cattail*. Aquatic insects: predaceous *diving beetles*, *dragon* and *damsel flies*, and of course *mosquitoes*! *Trout* populations expand many fold. *Green frogs* and their clan find a home.

A beaver pond is a mega-magnet to many kinds of wildlife. Beaver pond specialists among the ducks are mainly dabblers: the familiar *black duck*, *mallard*, *green-winged teal*, to which could be added the *wood duck* and the *hooded merganser*.

Some other feathered friends that like the pond are the *spotted sandpiper*, the *bittern*, the *great blue heron*, the *common snipe*, the *belted kingfisher* and the *tree swallow*. The *icterid* (blackbirds) as a group don't mind getting their feet wet; number among these the *rusty* and *red-winged blackbirds*, and the *common grackle*.

The *muskrat* has sometimes been called the beaver's poor cousin, an apt name, as this big mouse often moves in as emergent vegetation becomes established. If there's a buoyant population of muskrats, *mink* will be present to take a toll of... the young.

Moose along with other animals owe the beaver for providing some quality food. Our biggest *deer* seeks out aquatic vegetation, necessary for healthy sodium and other minerals, elements that are scant in birch twigs and fir foliage. *White-tails* aren't quite so obsessed with the wetland vegetation, yet they'll come around too.

Beavers are large enough that they don't have too many enemies; however, the *coyote* and the *bobcat* will make dinner out of a beaver if they catch it away from water. Maybe they appear slow and cumbersome, however beavers have formidable teeth and strong claws. Not swift on land, beavers come into their own in the water. They can, if necessary, stay submerged for a quarter of an hour and swim up to half a mile under water. Beavers have specialized adaptations to assist them in their work. A very useful one is the fur-lined lips that prevent unwanted intake of water when these guys carry sticks below the surface. Rare among mammals, beaver are often tolerant of non-blood relatives within the colony. They often mate for life, and are monogamous unless one of the pair goes permanently missing. The survivor will remate, thus explaining a significant age difference that biologists commonly detect between members of a pair.

Among the *woodpeckers*, the crow-sized *pileated* is a stand out. Its body size and strength are related to its food (carpenter ants) and where the ants live (large-boled spruces). Often deep in the trunk the carpenter ants are virtually impossible for other woodpeckers to obtain. Expert at wood hewing, the *pileated* simply chips out a deep slot, gaining access to its favourite food.

 The *pileated*'s nesting cavity, somewhere between 3¼ and 3½ inches in diameter, is fortunately (for other wildlife) only used by the maker for one year, then it's available to a long list of prospective "tenants." These cavities are the apartment of choice for *flying squirrel* families. *Pine martens* prefer them as apartments. Even *bats* that haven't managed to locate a suitable attic resort to one of these convenient homes. Among the birds to benefit are *wood ducks*, *hooded mergansers*, *common goldeneyes*, *kestrels*, *saw-whet owls* and *screech owls*. Other secondary cavity nesters (i.e., birds that aren't able to build their own homes but appreciate the "Log Cock's" generosity) are the *eastern bluebird*, the *tree swallow* and the *great crested flycatcher*. The useful life of the cavity will often reach 20 years, so it's a project that just keeps giving. If you added them up, it's nine species of birds that could be prospective tenants. As the cavity is used year after year the entrance becomes ever larger; eventually it can be suitable for a *barred owl*, a *common merganser*, or a *black duck.*

The *gaspereau*, a type of herring that enters freshwater to spawn, is extremely important in the food chain for waterborne wildlife. The "alewife," as it's sometimes called, while a bit bony for human palates, is eaten from the spring breakup right through early summer. The biggest bird that will add it to its menu is the *bald eagle*, followed by the *osprey*, the *common loon*, and the *double-crested cormorant.* If you'd enjoy watching cormorants and *harbour seals* in fishing mode, go to Falls View Park at the Reversing Falls Rapids on the lower St. John River. When the "sawbellys" (this is another name, and quite descriptive too) enter the smaller spawning streams, *raccoons*, *mink*, *otters*, and *great blue herons* join forces to try and diminish their number. Spawning complete, many of the adults weaken and die. In the meantime the fry become small minnow-sized fish, and when they start dropping down to the sea, they provide food for efficient fish catchers, like *common* and *red-breasted mergansers* and *common golden-eye*, besides the *loons* and *cormorants.*

9. Some Great Bays

Giant tides and the Bay of Fundy are synonymous. A happy accident of nature supports what happens: the Bay is a wedge both vertically and in the horizontal plane. Yet the most compelling force is that the length of the Bay, in harmonic terms, is just about perfect to be amplified by the main ocean tides. It works this way: the out-flowing tide collides with the incoming Atlantic Ocean tide at a critical time in the daily tidal rhythm. From Grand Manan, a gatekeeper island at the mouth of the Bay, where the difference is a respectable 16 feet or thereabouts, the tidal fluctuation becomes quite ridiculous (geographically) up at the mouth of the Petitcodiac where the number is about 40.

As if deliberately to complicate understanding, the tidal day is 24 hours and 50 minutes long, so over the span of a week, the timing of the high tide (or the low tide) will advance by about five hours from a Monday to a Saturday. So, for one to walk on the beach, fish from the wharf, or to kayak, attention has to be paid to the stage of the tides. Your very life could depend on paying attention.

Some folks, hearing about the Gulf Stream, which actually shuns the coast of Atlantic Canada, credit it at least in part with driving the tides. Not so. Logically, if such was the case, the water would be on the warm side, rather than being very frigid as it actually is. Bone chilling. The water is cold because of the constant mixing from top to bottom.

Water can hold more oxygen with decreasing temperature. This fact explains the tremendous biological productivity of the Bay. The name "Fundy," at least in one version, comes from a word meaning "profound," or "deep," in Portuguese. Relative to productivity, depth enhances upwelling, literally stirring the soup!

From the outer Bay to the top, where New Brunswick & Nova Scotia join, some of the more significant land and watermarks are:
(1) the Old Sow, a tidal whirlpool with awesome power at certain stages of the tide at the southern tip of Deer Island. It attracts pods of porpoises and seals, and in fall huge numbers of Bonaparte's gulls, which mainly eat shrimp.
(2) At the mouth of the St. John River we have the unique Reversing Falls Rapids. While not as high as Niagara, they perform feats much more dramatic than the honeymoon playground.

Rookeries of gulls and double-crested cormorants are established on islands in the stream, to afford access to the bounty of migrating fish. Harbour seals join in too.

As a tourist attraction, the Reversing Falls River is a magnet, offering passive viewing, sports kayaking and jet boating.

(3) Further up the Bay, almost to Moncton, we come to the giant, sandstone conglomerate "flower pots," which are nicely and precisely described in French as *Demoiselles.* A few pots of equivalent dimensions occur as isolated individuals, or a few in a group in other rock formations elsewhere, but 60 in a kilometer of shoreline!

(4) The Tidal Bore, a partner of the Old Sow mentioned earlier, has been diminished by causeways on the Petitcodiac, so to experience the best of this tidal feature one should go to the "Shubie" (Shubenacadie River) of Nova Scotia. If you're intrepid, try riding the incoming wave of water in a zodiac. Hint: leave your wallet and car keys on land!

As is the norm for cold, oxygen-enriched waters, what the Bay of Fundy lacks in diversity it makes up for in the quantities of what does occur. Plankton, the "pasture of the sea," may be present in millions of individuals in a cubic meter of water. Primitive plants (phytoplankton) are the engine of the system, but even the little animals (the zooplankton, small crabs, shrimp, and embryo fish) are important in the stew of life. To fully appreciate the beauty of items afloat, low magnification would help, especially for the plant portion of the stew.

Mud shrimp, about the length of the pin that holds a ladies' watch strap in place, have been calculated to peak in early August at 60,000 per square meter in the flats at the head of the Bay. No wonder this area is a fuelling stop for flocks of sandpipers, easily numbering 100,000 in a flock. The small ones are lumped together as peep.

Fishery scientists have determined that, on the incoming tide, temperature sensitive shad that have come here all the way from Cape Cod find the feeding extremely good. A sort of super herring, shad have large mouths which they hold open as they swim along in schools many thousand strong. A prime food is the mysid shrimp.

A sunny warm July in any year will ensure a bounty for adult fish, sea birds, on up to whales the following season, even if the same month a year later is cold and foggy. This is reflected in the abundance of shearwaters, petrels, and phalaropes, and even in the numbers of great whales lingering around Deer, Campobello, and the Grand Manan group of islands. Life pulses, sometimes slowly, sometimes with a faster beat, but always with a beat.

A good way to fully appreciate the true character of the Bay is to join an organized beach walk with an interpreter-naturalist of the Atlantic Coastal Action Program at Fundy National Park, St. Andrews, or west Saint John. A group of a couple of dozen participants will often represent a good cross section of society. Some may never have been on the shore before; others may have been born within a few miles. The latter group will be looking for subtleties. For example, they'll compare the size of rough periwinkles; they're the ones that hardly ever get wet because they live at the head of the tide.

Although folks are encouraged <u>not</u> to collect the shellfish, children can't resist. A periwinkle here, a whelk there, it all adds up. When you tally up the hundreds of people that wander the inter-tidal zone during the 100-day local summer, the take is significant.

A sauntering pace suddenly picks up when the naturalist finds something unusual, maybe a stranded goosefish. Black, big headed with serious dental equipment, the goosefish, it is said, can swallow a goose in one gulp. This is fanciful, as its regular mode of operation is to lie inconspicuously on the bottom in deep water and wait, and wait. Sometimes it displays its antennae-like lure, confirming it as a member of the angler fish family. Main meals are other fish. Any hopelessly stranded and expiring goosefish will become lunch for a bald eagle, or a gang of gulls.

We're now approaching the so-called bottom of the tide. If a full moon is imminent and the tides especially low, we may see some unusual creatures. The naturalist has a few favourite tidal pools. In one of them, pie-sized sea stars lurk. And there's sea anenomes, sedentary animals, not plants at all.

Here on the Fundy shore there's dulse, an edible seaweed. A brochure claims 27 important vitamins and minerals. These plants grow bountifully and are harvested commercially on the shores of Grand Manan. One of the visitors holds up something else that superficially looks like a plant. It's beige, like cheap paper towel, and many lobed. Again, it's identified. To the surprise of most, it's called hornwrack, and it's a simple community of animals.

Rummaging around in another pool, the naturalist pulls out a palm sized green crab. It's not very threatening. In earlier times, there would have been lobsters in-shore in such situations. Efficient utilization in the commercial fishery sees that this doesn't happen in these days. Presence of these guys would encourage a bit more care in reaching in blindly.

The tide turns. It can come over the flats at about a foot per minute. It's time to go back. A mid-morning breeze picks up, calling up a Fundy region expression: "You don't always need your sweater, but if you're wise you always know its whereabouts!"

Information on the inter-tidal zone of Northumberland Strait is available at Kouchibouquac National Park, where there is an excellent Visitor Centre.

La Dune Buctouche Visitor Centre and boardwalk is an excellent site from which to explore three elements of the Northumberland-Kent shore: the seashore; a pristine dune complex, the most expansive north of Cape Cod; and a sheltered brackish lagoon.

Further north, we find the Bay of Chaleur in the Campbellton-Dalhousie area. This feature is really misnamed. The first European explorer pointed his ship into the Bay during a heat wave in June! It's mostly ice in winter, with open stretches being utilized by the most hardy of ducks, like the Barrow's and common goldeneyes.

All the bays along New Brunswick's "North Shore" have something that the coast of the Bay of Fundy has only in short supply. We're talking here of islands and sand beaches. Many of the islands harbour nesting birds. Heron

Island off Charlo is home to birds of the same name. In Miramichi Bay there are several islands in the 1.0 kilometer length range: Bay du Vin, Fox and Portage. All these islands are distinct biologically.

The shoreline from Tracadie-Sheila south is extremely important in the recovery efforts directed towards the endangered piping plover. Besides the beaches protected by Kouchibouquac National Park, and the Eco-centre at Buctouche, some important beaches are in the Neguac-Tabisintac areas. A specific group is striving to protect and conserve the "piper." In a couple of years they have seen the plover populations stabilize or grow.

10. Where the Mermaids Play

In theory, the sea is full of fish. Correction: it was once that way. What still applies is the intimate knowledge of fishermen and others that gain their livelihood from the oceans. To a landsman, a herring might be a commercially important fish. To a full-time fisherman, it's possible to identify the life stages starting with the egg/spawn, which is followed by the fry, and then the brit (one below the sardine), which is still only about a third the length of a full-sized herring.

Fish of the sea fall into two major categories: *groundfish* (which swim near the bottom) and *pelagics* (which take to the open sea). *Cod* is a classic groundfish. Its associates are *haddock*, *hake* and *pollock*. Neighbours are *flounder* and *halibut*. These last two really hug the bottom, real bottom feeders!

Pelagics live well above the bottom in the water

column, and may even appear on the surface, especially at night. They're sociable and tend to travel in large schools. *Herring, shad* and *mackerel* are a few representatives.

An unlikely mermaid in almost anyone's assessment is the *walrus*, and it did once occur, at least sparingly, in the Bay of Fundy. This has been confirmed by the occasional skull recovered in fishing gear. Better candidates for mermaids would be the *seals*. The *harbour seal* is positively appealing, unless you have aquaculture cages full of salmon! This segment of the fishery calls these small seals by a less than appealing name; to them they're "rock maggots." In common parlance, the harbour seal is often called a "sea dog." At times, they do bark enthusiastically. Sea Dog Cove situated on the Kennebecasis River is still to this day a favourite haunt. Sometimes the mothers whelp on the outer islets at the mouth of the cove. Unlike the more northern "ice" seals, the pups of the harbour seal can swim when only a few days old, and do not have the luxury of lolling about and being super-charged with high-energy seal milk for nearly a fortnight. Being in more southern waters, harbour seals couldn't rely on a platform of ice for birthing. Also threatened by a greater range of predators, including man, they have adapted by having their young develop early precociousness. When I was a youngster, my dad sometimes would invite me to join him for an evening paddle in the family canoe. Particularly if it was a bit foggy or misty, we'd often be joined by a harbour seal. They were so curious that they would often circle us as we paddled along. Popping up, revealing head and shoulders, they did, as Dad suggested, look a lot like a bewhiskered old man. This appearance led to the obvious label for a senior sailor, an "old sea dog."

The *grey seal* grows to about three times the bulk of the *harbour seal.* Big males go up to about 600 lbs. They are the second most common seal in the Bay of Fundy. The grey seal summers along the Northumberland Strait, and pods of 40 or 50 are common along the outer bars at Kouchibouquac National Park. They are occasional around the islets of the Grand Manan archipelago. Harbour and grey often haul out together. Besides size and a greyer fur in the grey, they have a distinctive head profile, leading to the local name of "horsehead."

Recently there have been reports in the Bay of Fundy of two species of seals associated with the north and ice. These are the *harp* and the *hood.* The harp is roughly the size of the harbour seal, while the hood is similar in size to the grey. Why are these animals arriving with increasing frequency in Bay of Fundy waters? The obvious answer is that they are spilling over from their booming populations near the core of their ranges. Or, they could simply be reclaiming "former" territory. Let's hope it's not as one wag put it: we're becoming more like the Arctic!

A Whale Watching Trip

We're at Seal Cove, the most southern community on Grand Manan. With a smile and an extended hand for those who need help, Durlan Ingersoll helps tour people that have booked to go out whale and seabird watching to board the 40 foot "Seawatcher." He's mate with Captain Peter Wilcox, owner-operator of the "Seawatcher." Following the lobster season the boat is fitted for "touring."

Durlan gives the visitors a run-down on the tides and

what was seen on the last trip out. Peter, who has been out of sight in the wheelhouse getting the boat checked out, pops out and explains the procedure with personal flotation devices and other safety equipment.

Today we'll be headed "outside" of Whitehead Island, as the tide is still falling. As Peter revs up the Volvo engine, he smoothly swings the "Seawatcher" about and we're away. Passengers check their camera gear and install long lenses. People in the know put blankets over their knees; "It's always colder offshore than on the land." That's true, like about 10 degrees Celsius cooler, on average.

Chugging along to the throb of the diesel, we pass work boats used in salmon aquaculture, barges with pile drivers, a couple of pleasure yachts. Then the "Seawatcher" starts to rise and fall with wind enhanced waves. While all this is proceeding, Durlan points out loafing eiders and cormorants on the small islands we pass. There's a bunch of harbour seals, some in the water, some hauled out. One loafer is larger and lighter in colour, a grey.

Someone spots a roosting mature bald eagle. On the water, guillemots in jet black suits, and with carmine legs and feet, batter out of the way. Off to the port there's a common loon in non-breeding plumage. Gulls check us out in an uninterested fashion. A few graceful terns, most probably of the Arctic type, dart about.

Peter also hosts trips to Seal Island as he calls it, where thousands of terns and hundreds of puffins nest. As the ownership of this island is contested (Canada and the US), Peter apparently doesn't like to use the name Machias

(Seal) Island, as Machias is a Maine place name.

Besides setting course, Peter has been hailing Dana Russell, another tour-boat captain, on the radio. Dana sails out of North Head, which is closer to the Grand Manan Channel, and is farther out than Peter. He reports a fog bank in the vicinity of the most likely area for the "rights." Reference here is to the North Atlantic right whale, which, while extremely rare, is most dependably seen off Grand Manan compared to the rest of the Atlantic seaboard. Rights are what the paying customers have come from the U.K., California, and Ontario to see.

The "Seawatcher" suddenly veers to the right, starboard in nautical terms. Peter has spotted a small pod of "fins" (finbacks, the second largest whales in the ocean, one below the blue) moving south. Our cruising speed, of about 8 or 9 knots, won't touch these greyhounds of the sea when they open up at about 20 knots. As they're feeding they aren't marathoning, so we get to see and enjoy them as they take a couple of dives. Cameras click as the fins disappear into the vastness of the sea.

As the watermen say, we still have about an hour's "steam" to reach the whales, so Durlan breaks out the bait bucket, takes his place on the stern, unsheathes his working knife, and begins chopping up small sardine herring. He tosses a couple of pieces in a high arc out over the wake. Predictably a herring gull makes a tight circle and swoops in, but before it can grab the prize the fish sinks into the depths. More gulls, including a ponderous great black-backed gull, show up. Durlan shakes his head. Like most commercial fishermen, he's not a lover of gulls.

Suddenly a long-winged greater shearwater zeros in on the wake. A gull tries to elbow it out of the way. It's then that the shearwater uses a strategy unavailable to the gulls; it dives. It rises with the bait and veers off to be replaced by more of its kind that are softly protesting among themselves; the greaters, with their gray bodies and distinctive black caps, are now joined by a few slightly smaller chocolate brown, sooty shearwaters. While all this commotion is proceeding, single gannets come in and circle the speeding boat at a distance. A few Wilson's storm petrels flutter by, and on a patch of floating seaweed a small group of phalaropes rests.

Right on our traverse, a large object comes vertically out of the water and then falls back in a mass of foam. Whale? No, Peter I.D.s it as a basking shark. They're here for the same reason as the rights, a feast of plankton. It's not long before we are alerted to the triangular fin that is the mark of one of these great creatures. Peter eases the boat alongside. Passengers can make out the black and mottled form of a 28-foot-long fish, swimming steadily and unwaveringly.

We're getting close to the whales. A lone hump-backed whale produces a spectacular breach. Its approximately 40 tonne body is vaulted clear of the surface. Durlan jokingly calls it by an alternate name: "clown of the sea."

Again Peter alters course. Dana's boat, "Against the Wind," is coming towards us. Its red hull shines cheerfully in the sun; the morning vapor has dissipated. The two captains are homing in on a courtship group of rights. There is at least one female, and as Durlan says with a grin, she's given the call. Bull rights are coming from all points of the compass. They aren't fast, perhaps a little more speedy than the lobster boat. Soon there's a dozen or more churning the water. The female, who has a largely white belly, is identified by name in the identification guide provided the commercial fishermen by the Whale and Seabird Research Station at North Head. Cameras click, and then, as suddenly as it started, it's over. The rights start feeding again.

A couple of animals pass across the stern. Not only can we hear their breathing, we get a whiff of the exhaled breath. It's an unpleasant oily odour.

When a great tail fluke goes strongly vertical, a deep dive is planned.

Peter points out that a 35 foot long right will go a ton per foot, so we don't want to get too cozy. The human cargo on the "Seawatcher" would weigh about 1/10 of a typical right whale.

We spend another hour circling slowly. Sometimes Peter "shuts down" (stops the engine) so as not to startle a nearby whale. More great views, more photos. When Dana comes close, all hands are waving, and calling out. It's been a fine trip, and no one sea sick as yet.

When we turn for the last time, Peter hauls the throttle back. The "Seawatcher's" bow rises. Some of the folks take out lunches and munchies. Hot chocolate comes up from the galley. Shearwaters with their stiff-winged flight angle across our path. One puffin and then another buzzes by with swift wing beats. A large brown bodied seabird that looks like an immature gull appears, but Durlan, always alert, discerns the marks of a jaeger. Ken Edwards, a longtime summer resident who often goes on these trips, confirms: a pomarine jaeger. This bird domineers the gulls, actually forcing one to disgorge. The jaeger drops to the waves grabbing its "prize."

Whitehead Island appears clearly on the starboard. Peter takes a shortcut to the harbour, as now the tide is high enough that he can safely take the inside passage between this island and Cheney Island. Durlan takes a turn at the wheel while Peter collects fares. As we swing into the wharf, a bald eagle soars over. The completion of a perfect day, and one that will be recalled with pleasure.

11. Actors, Impersonators, Deceivers

For our animal friends, impersonation nor deception is punishable in one of our courts of law! We're the ones carrying the moral baggage. For wildlife it's all about individual survival and the perpetuation of the species. The general rule is, if it works, someone will do it!

A *raven* living in an area where *coyotes* and *wolves* were being poisoned found a "clean" carcass. On hearing a group of his kind noisily winging toward him, he quickly flipped over on his back, feigning death. He righted himself and became a healthy raven when his mate appeared.

Crows do some pretty smart things too, like conning wandering dogs into ripping open garbage bags so they can get some easy pickin's.

The smaller *blue jay*, a member of the same family as the crow and the raven, practices a unique deception. To clear a feeding tray of competing birds like *starlings* and *grosbeaks*, the blue jay will come roaring in doing a creditable rendition of the scream of the *red-tailed hawk*. It always works!

If you count camouflage as deception, there are lots of examples from the natural world. Spotted *white-tail* fawns are virtually invisible among sun dappled vegetation. They have at least two things going for them: they are obedient and stay still, and at a young age they have virtually no scent.

Hares and *weasels* change pelage (fur) colour to adjust to the seasons.

Many birds are camouflaged, especially when immature. Some birds have their outlines broken up by having black bars against a white chest, as is the case with several species of *plover*. This is disruptive visually to a potential predator, and works in concert with camouflage. Most birds that place their eggs open to the sky have developed visually confusing patterns of scrolls, streaks and spots to decorate these eggs. Many shorebirds don't build much of a nest, hardly more than a scraped depression. Often the eggs can't be visually separated from the associated pebbles, even from close proximity. Very clever, and it also works!

Just about everyone, from a disturbed *sphinx moth* caterpillar to an upset *great horned owl* will try to make themselves more frightening by increasing their apparent size, a form of bluffing. *Black bears*, when they perform that rare charge, will puff themselves up. Hardly necessary to put the fear in most of us!

A classic case of mimicry or impersonation is the safe-to-eat (for most birds) *vicerory butterfly* mimicking the *monarch* in colour and wing pattern. The monarch is poisonous to all small birds.

Not only does the *American bittern* have striped plumage, when approached it compresses its thin body, pointing its bill to the sky. If there's a breeze the already convincing bird will rock back and forth with the swaying marsh grass.

Male *northern harriers* will try to maximize their gene flow to succeeding generations by practicing a form of deceit. Males arrive on the home territory before the females. When the first potential mate shows up, the male will present her with gifts of mice. If mice are abundant, when she establishes a nest and begins laying, he'll try and court a second female with the same procedure. If a third unattached female appears, the same performance will be repeated. Field biologists haven't (as yet) detected bigamy extending to more than three wives!

In a reverse situation to the harrier the female *spotted sandpiper* does a number on her mate or mates. She and the first mate she chooses pick a nest site, build a nest, and the female lays a clutch of eggs. Then the female bows out, leaving the incubation job to the daddy. This female will then train as many males as come around, up to the number five. Like a score in a hockey match, it looks like the female spotty at 5 has it over the cock harrier at 3!

The *brown-headed cowbird* (alternately called buffalo bird) is the premier nest parasite of North American birds. It's been recorded dropping eggs in the nests of over 100 species of birds. These eggs are well designed, as they hatch a few days ahead of the host's own eggs. The cowbird is amazingly able to fairly well duplicate the egg colour and pattern of the host eggs. The cowbird does have an alibi, though; as when following the wanderings of the *buffalo* across miles of prairie, they couldn't stop and complete a nesting cycle of several weeks. The cowbird hung around buffalo, and nowadays hangs around cows, because of the insects on their big warm bodies plus the ones these large footed animals stir up as they walk.

Reactions to the intrusion of the cowbird vary. *Robins* and *catbirds* throw the offending egg out. *Yellow warblers* build a new nest over whatever eggs are already present, including their own. They sacrifice. In some cases the victimized bird simply abandons the nest.

Among the ducks, the hen *redhead* is a sneak,

habitually dropping eggs in other ducks' nests. At least she can't be accused of putting all her eggs in one basket! Cavities for ducks that seek them out are at a premium in many localities. This could be the reason why the *hooded merganser*, the *wood duck* and the *common goldeneye* sometimes deposit eggs in each other's nests. All done surreptitiously of course, in the best spirit of deception!

12. Feathered Guilds

After the nesting season, the vigorously defended territory of the forest perching bird dissolves, and animosities so prevalent when a nest and young are at stake vanish. Gradually everyone becomes tolerant again. It's then that busy little troupes of *black-capped chickadees, ruby-crowned* and *golden-crowned kinglets, black-throated green warblers*, a *brown creeper*, or two, a couple of *nuthatches*, and perhaps a *downy* or a *hairy woodpecker* appear. This guild of "tradesmen" is an efficient way to utilize the resources of the forest, as each brings to the group specialized skills that are unique to its species.

Warblers, and the black-throated green is only one of them, pick caterpillars from leaves at the tips of branches, or flycatch between tree crowns.

 The *chickadees*, with their strong legs, are able to hang upside down while inspecting the under side of branches for adult and immature insects.

Kinglets cover some of the same territory by hovering underneath branches and foliage.

Redstarts are also proficient at flycatching.

Spiraling up tree trunks is the style of the thin-billed *brown creeper*. With its stiff tail for propping itself, it has some of the characteristics of a woodpecker. The down-curved thin bill is designed for prying insects from under flakes of bark.

Taking a reverse direction, both the *red* and *white-breasted nuthatches* inspect tree trunks by starting at the crown and working down!

Both *downy* and *hairy woodpeckers* share things too. The smaller downy restricts itself to small branches, whereas the hairy zeros in on larger branches and tree trunks.

Sometimes *gray jays* furtively flit around the edges of a slowly moving mixed flock. They may be attracted out of curiosity.

Others on the fringes are a bit more sinister. A sharp-shinned hawk, hearing the contact calls between guild members, is apt to streak in for a meal. If it's spotted before an attack, the group goes completely silent.

Not a daytime creature, a seven inch high *saw whet owl* monitors the activity from the security of his hollow stub of a tree. He will project the guild's location by dusk, when he'll go hunting. He'd be happy with our New Brunswick Provincial Bird, the black-capped chickadee, for supper.

Yellow-bellied sapsuckers are woodpeckers that in summer feed mainly on the liquid sap they steal from white birches, red maples and apple trees. They do this by drilling shallow holes, really minature wells, in long parallel rows up and down the trunk. Very early in the sap flow, many sweet-loving flies and other insects are attracted to the tasty liquid. Making its rounds later, the sapsucker savours them along with the sap.

Any *hummingbirds* in the area will visit this informal feeding station. *Warblers*, *hermit* and *Swainson's thrushes* will visit, too. Red squirrels will stop for a sip during daylight hours. After dark *flying squirrels* are not to be outdone by their red-pelaged brothers, and they also visit. The sapsucker tree acts like a magnet for a whole array of wildlife, and does provide us with an interesting guild.

Let's leave the shelter of the forest and visit a field being turned over by the plough. Very quickly, *ring-billed gulls* and *crows* gather to feast on worms and any beetles that haven't found cover. If it rains and worms stay out, a *wood turtle* may emerge from the nearby hardwood forest to enjoy them as a meal!

Another guild involves both birds and mammals. Visit the *Reversing Falls Rapids* in Saint John at any time other than slack water. *Herring gulls* and *blackbacks* wheel and scream even during the winter months. From spring into summer and fall, *double-crested cormorants* ride the downstream and upstream turbulence, fishing all the while. When they surface with a prize – a *gaspereau*, a *smelt*, or *herring* – any nearby herring gull will attempt theivery. Sometimes the great black-backed gull dominates the scene. In the middle of all this activity, *harbour seals* bob and dive.

On warm summer evenings, especially after the middle of August, *ants* swarm in millions, intent on mating and then establishing new colonies. This is too much for any sharp-eyed *herring gulls* and *ring-billed gulls* in the vicinity to resist. They present a strange spectacle as they glide and bank, grabbing at an ant or ants. Other than feel sorry for the victims, observers have to admire the flying skills. Just at dusk the gulls retire, to be replaced by the *nighthawks*, skilled aerial insect catchers. Then, as darkness falls, little *brown bats* take over.

The little band of inquisitive chickadees and friends mentioned earlier, in their wanderings, may well find your bird feeding station. The core of this group will be the *chickadees*, mostly *black-capped* but possibly *boreal* chickadees as well if you live north of Fredericton. Both the *red-breasted* and *white-breasted nuthatches* will be there; the *golden-crowned kinglets*, the friendly little *downy woodpecker*, and if you're very lucky, occasionally the elusive *brown creeper*.

Not part of the original guild, but now joining the feeder contingent as summer draws to an end are a whole raft of *sparrows*: the *tree*, the *white-throated*, maybe the *song* and the *fox.*

Another "sparrow" that's dependable is the *dark-eyed junco.* From New England south, it's earned the honour of being called "snow bird." In our clime we reserve this label for the snow bunting.

Then the ubiquitous *blue jays*, almost everybody's feeder favourite? If your home is in the softwoods, or near an extensive forest stand, you may have *gray jays*, too. They'll always defer to blue jays.

Besides the predatory *sharp-shinned hawk*, that once it finds a feeder visited by small birds will tend to come back, we certainly can expect visits from any *northern shrikes* in the neighbourhood. These gray jay look-alikes are most interested in chickadees, yet, if really hungry, may attempt a larger sparrow.

13. On Being Hawklike

In southern New Brunswick, if we try fairly hard, we can identify at least 17 species of day-flying raptors, or birds of prey. Add to this eight species of night-flying owls.

Raptors range all the way from the jay-sized *northern shrike* to the *bald eagle* with a body as big as a turkey. No matter how much effort we expend, we won't be able to see all of the raptors at any one season of the year. *Broad-winged hawks* and *ospreys*, for example, are summer residents only. The cold-tolerant *rough-legged hawk* is a winter visitor, often joined by the *snowy owl*, which has never nested this far south. Some others, the *gyrfalcons* and some of the merlins, are birds of passage. The *bald eagle*, our largest in the group, is a confirmed year-round resident. Largest maybe, but not the most fierce; that title without question goes to the "tiger of the woods," the *great horned owl*. This, our largest owl, has a wing span of about four feet, against the eagle's eight.

Some raptors soar a lot. The falcon family are able not only to fly fast but to maintain their speed for a considerable distance. Falcon wings are pointed, and being a bit delicate aren't suitable for going through bushes, or for contact with tree branches. The owl equivalent of the falcons is the *hawk owl*. This long-winged and long-tailed bird often hunts on cloudy days. Our three *accipters* have evolved to hunt through the trees. Their short rounded wings combined with a long tail give them ultra manouverability. They can, if necessary, put on a burst of speed, yet aren't capable of sustained flight at top speed.

Besides not getting a lot of exposure to raptors because of their relative rarity, there are other problems for the field person with this group:
1. They tend to be shy and wary of people, even very elusive, as with most owls.
2. Even within a species there can be quite a bit of variation in size and in plumage colouration.
3. Many fly quite fast, or quite high, or both!

Other than family groups at the end of the breeding season, hawks don't regularly congregate in very large numbers, with the following exceptions: the hardy *rough-legs*, a *buteo* or soaring type hawk about half the size of an eagle, will concentrate in intervale or meadow land in winter provided the snow does not go over a foot deep. These birds are mouse specialists. It's possible to see upwards of 20 to 25 in a day at either of the following preferred locations: the Tantramar border area between New Brunswick and Nova Scotia, and the intervale flood plain south of Fredericton, between Maugerville and Jemseg, including Sheffield.

The winter meadows of the border area and the Sepody marshes of Albert County are the best places for the *snowy owl*. In these preferred areas it's possible to see upwards of a half dozen during incursion winters. They happen about every six years.

Our smallest buteo is the *broad-winged hawk*. It's also our commonest. After mid-August and into early September, on warm afternoons with good thermals, it's possible to witness casual-looking migration along east-west ridges in the southern region. Kettles of ten to twelve soaring birds would be excellent. To put this into some sort of perspective, around a thousand birds a day often pass over Hawk Mountain, PA from mid to late September. For this species migration is quite leisurely.

The *broad-winged*'s hunting technique consists of low energy and quiet perching on an elevated stub of a tree, watching the surrounding environment. Pity any small *vole* or *mouse*, or newly fledged bird that comes within the view-shed. Broad-wings often take *frogs* and are good at handling *garter snakes*. They grab snakes by the head, creating quite a visual image as they fly off with the disabled snake swinging below. It would be best, don't you think, if the nestlings didn't ask too many questions about what's for dinner?

The *red-tailed*, and the *red-shouldered hawks* are about the same size, yet are quite different in a number of ways. First, habitat: the *red-tail* prefers rolling country, open fields surrounded by mature forest; the *red-shoulder* likes wet, poorly drained woodlands. It eats much the same foods as the broad-wing. A mouser, and a rodent specialist, the red-tail will take a hare if it gets the chance. Also red and gray squirrels are preferred foods. It won't turn down a ruffed grouse or a pheasant either!

Our second smallest hawk, the *sharp-shin* is a forest hawk, and as an accipiter is well adapted in this environment. At 9 to 13 inches, only the *kestrel*, a *falcon*, is smaller. These small hawks are in the size range of the *saw whet* and the *boreal* owls. All four prefer small birds as prey.

Our other common accipter is the *goshawk*, a very able and serious hawk, although it's unlikely that many of them can live up to their name: literally, "goose" hawk. It's raven-sized. Prey is quite variable: birds up to the bulk of a *ruffed grouse*, also *squirrels*, *hares*, *woodchucks*, and smaller mammals like *voles* and *mice*. Goshawks are notably fierce. A woodsman from Albert County told me of a goshawk that captured a mink and was in the act of transporting it. The mink hadn't completely expired, and in a final desperate move bit the hawk's throat. Both came tumbling to earth. On checking for survivors, he found that nobody won; both prey and predator were dead!

While the *American kestrel*, a *falcon*, is quite tiny, being about the bulk of a *blue jay* and certainly smaller than most of us visualize a hawk, it's our most colourful hawk, being orange on the back and having bluish wings. From its classic power-line perch, it flies direct to a *cricket* or *grasshopper*, a small *mouse*, or small bird. If fine-tuning is required it will skillfully hover.

Next up in size in the clan falcon is the *merlin*. In many ways it behaves as a small *peregrine*, eating from the same groups of prey, just choosing smaller examples. Skilled at tail-chasing its potential prey, or flying fast and low and screened to the last minute, it depends on surprise to capture its unsuspecting prey.

Peregrine means "wanderer," and this name suits the ultimate falcon. This hawk is the fastest thing in feathers. Its typical hunting mode is to tower at a good elevation, then power stoop at over 100 miles per hour. Targets are mainly other birds: *flickers*, *robins*, *blue jays*, shorebirds and smaller ducks. The peregrine doesn't tolerate unwelcome visitors around an active nest. With clenched talons it can knock the "stuffing" out a raven that unwisely comes too close.

Nesting north of us, the *gyrfalcon* shows up some winters. Larger than the Peregrine Falcon, it can take any duck, not just the smaller ones.

The *osprey*, just one species world-wide, is in character like the beaver in the mammal world. It works hard, doesn't waste time on aggression, and is occasionally taken advantage of. The "fish hawk" is nearly exclusively a fish eater

– all kinds of fish: *gaspereau*, *shad*, *herring* and *suckers*. Ospreys are among the most sociable of hawks, and if food is plentiful, they'll tolerate neighbours nearby. Practical to a fault, they like to nest as near to the fishing grounds as possible. Preferably the female will be able to see her mate fishing while she's incubating. It's a team effort after all. The *bald eagle*, well equipped to feed itself, will pirate away an osprey's catch if given a chance. Hardly fair, when you consider the load-bearing osprey being assaulted by an attacker 25 to 30% larger.

To the layperson, confusion can be caused by the plumages of the *northern harrier*. Bluish gray to silvery is the hue of the male. The female is dark brown. A likely assumption would be two species. Harriers quarter over wet meadows, mainly looking for meadow *voles*. Besides superb sight, their hearing is also well-developed; they possess facial discs to enhance sound collection. The harrier does the day shift, and the *short-eared owl*, also a fine mouser, attends to the nights. This medium sized owl conjures up an image of a mid-sized bat as it flies along with loping, somewhat moth-like flight.

Leave it to our largest raptor to be about the shrewdest. The *bald eagle* won't expend any unnecessary energy. Watchful waiting is an effective strategy for the big fellows. It's got to be an easy meal or an eagle won't bother. Rather a freshly dead fish than one you have to capture.

Two eagles co-operated in the taking of an eider duckling. Eagle no. 1 flew over a hen eider and her family of two. The ducks dove as the eagle flew around for another pass. Eagle no. 2 came from a different direction, and when the frightened family bobbed to the surface, grabbed one of the ducklings. This episode was witnessed by Eileen Pike and friends in July, 2002, at the beach at Anchorage Provincial Park on Grand Manan.

Suspected of nesting sporadically in the higher hills in the Big Woods of northern New Brunswick, the *golden eagle*, unlike the bald eagle is a "super hawk." A new deer fawn wouldn't be beyond the competence of one of these birds. Goldens have been flown successfully against wolves in the Asian desert. Golden eagles don't eat rotting fish or any other carrion unless starving!

The *great horned owl*, besides hunting down other owls, catches *skunks* and may, ill-advisedly of course, go after a *porcupine*. They're *hare* specialists, and often in winter catch *grouse* budding in the hardwood crowns, especially if these wild chickens persist in staying out into the dusk. Not picky eaters, the great horned will not turn down a *frog*, and if a fish jumps clear of a pond surface when the owl is traversing, it will likely be caught.

Next in size to the great horned is the brown-eyed, *earless barred owl*. Not as aggressive as its yellow-eyed competitor, the barred still does very well in New Brunswick. Its trade mark, "who cooks for you, who cooks for you alllllllll............" has been heard by many people. It preys mostly on small mammals: *squirrels*, *mice*, and young *hares*. It shows restraint when it spots a porcupine!

All the *owls* are incapable of fashioning a proper nest, a problem they get around very nicely

by simply commandeering a hollow stub, or an unused stick nest, or a *pileated* or *flicker* cavity.

The *great horned* widens its choice of sites by nesting early, often taking over *red-tailed hawk* nests, or old *crow* and *raven* nests. On time for these guys is February or March, early for the *red-tail*, that will have to build a new nest later in the spring. The great horned has an elaborate courtship ritual, feasible as they don't have to go to the trouble of building a nest from scratch.

The *long-eared owl* often nests, like its bigger look-alike, in abandoned nests of other birds. The *short-eared* uses the marsh swards as cover for a nest on the ground. The little *saw whet* is happy with a *pileated* cavity.

Not "foul and ghastly" at all, the *turkey vulture* is part of a skilled clean-up crew. They have seen the bounty of road-killed *raccoons*, *woodchucks*, *snakes* and *hares*, and followed it to the north. That dihedral wing profile is now a given every summer in southern N.B. This vulture has an exceptional sense of smell. Experiments have shown that with warm air currents wafting upward, the turkey vulture is able to zero-in on the odour of a mouse under a man-high hay cock. This vulture prefers a diet of mammals and birds.

The *black vulture*, still a rarity in N.B., generally stays coastal as it prefers "ripe" fish. The nearly featherless heads of both vultures are an adaptation that aides cleanliness.

Crows, *ravens* and *jays* aren't raptors, but they're predatory in some of their behavioral traits, and they're darn good at scavenging. Until the *turkey vulture* came north, the crows and ravens had the road kill fallout all to themselves. Crows will lead sharp-clawed and sharp-toothed dogs to your curbside garbage bag so they'll rip it open, so all hands will be able to sample the "goodies" therein. Ravens, more attuned to the wilderness than their smaller brothers, have been recorded leading a wolf pack to a moose bogged in deep snow. After the kill the raven can benefit by participating in the cleanup.

Ravens will visit a saltmarsh just as the spring tides are peaking. Pity the poor *vole* isolated on a small grass tussock and afraid to swim! I've seen a raven gobble up half a dozen in a few minutes under such a situation. *Crows* will gather in a hay field as the mower goes on its rounds. They will be joined by *gulls* on a *grasshopper* feast, and any tasty young *mice* that become exposed!

If the *blue jay* is the extrovert, as most will agree, the deep woods *gray jay* is an introvert. In spite of apparant shyness the gray fellow quickly learns to benefit from man. The report of a rifle will bring him out of seclusion. Another sure way is to light a lunch fire in the spruce woods. Whether it's noise of gathering fuel or the visual of that heavenward wisp of smoke that attracts them is an open question.

Our cunning friend is among the earliest nesters in the north woods. The only active nests that I've found were located in March, when the snow lay deep upon the ground. The walls of the nest are thick and the whole thing is quite bulky, considering the adults are about robin-sized. Nest as they do under marginal conditions, the structure has been developed to be well insulated. Ecologically a good move, this early off the mark nesting has the young jays on the wing when other perching birds are at the height of their nesting activity – lots of fresh eggs and helpless nestlings for these marauders to sample.

The *shrikes* we most often see show up in the winter months. These "northerns" have nested in Labrador and Ungava. Generally travelling singly they are the scourge of feeders, capturing everything from *chickadees* to *juncos*. Any food that is beyond immediate needs is impaled on a thorn or wedged in a crotch of a branch, leading to an alternate name of "butcher bird." They do look sinister in their gray plumage with a black mask, even though they are not much bigger than a jay.

14. A Beach Lover's Scene

Sandpipers dominate the shore. *Gulls* too are significant players. Often solitary in style are the *herons*.

Over 30 species of *sandpipers* spend part of the year in New Brunswick. Most of these are migrants. A few species migrate through in the spring on the way to the vast Arctic breeding grounds. Many more kinds spend time with us in the late summer or fall on the passage to winter quarters.

Only the *purple sandpiper* is a dependable winter resident. This sturdy, short legged fellow frequents surf-washed breakwaters and exposed headlands in small flocks from Saint John Harbour west. Point Lepreau, Maces Bay, and Chance Harbour are good sites. It can spend the winter months this far north because the giant tides don't permit much ice to form on the shore.

There is no standard sandpiper. Members of this clan range in size from about that of a small sparrow to the body size of a duck. Most have long bills designed for probing.

The *plovers*, an exception to the rule, have short rigid bills for picking food from the surface. Most have long pointed wings making fast flight or great journeys possible and feasible.

An exception is the forest dwelling *woodcock* that has rounded wings to make navigation in its obstacle-filled environment easier.

All of this group have precocious young, and the norm is four large eggs to a clutch. In some species, in which the female is larger than the male, all the incubating is done by her. Her advantage is in bulk, an adaptation to maximize egg size relative to body size.

In a few species the sex roles seem a bit odd. Our familiar bum-bobbing *spotted sandpiper* that nests along most river beaches and the shores of larger ponds, fools most when it comes to family responsibilities. Slightly larger, the female is more aggressive than the male and has him assist with nest site selection and building. It's a bit more elaborate than that of most of the group: a grass, moss and even feather-lined cradle. It's just as well that the male participates in this phase, as it's likely he'll be doing all the incubation. He'll be basically doing nothing but sitting for 20 days or more. He's the original "Mr. Mom!" In the meantime, the female courts another male and repeats the whole performance. If surplus males are available, and there's lots of food, she may have up to five mates throughout the summer.

The lobe-footed, often swimming *phalaropes* have taken the sex reversal role even further. Not only does the female delegate incubation to the male, she also leaves all the post-hatch care to the male. In all three North American phalaropes, the females are physically larger and noticeably more colourful than their mates. Only one, the *Wilson's pond nester*, raises its family here in New Brunswick.

The mud flats of the upper Bay of Fundy are very important to south-bound shorebirds in the fall. So vital is the energy boost to some species, especially a whole group of small sandpipers collectively labeled "peep," that up to 90% of the continental population can be found gorging on the abundant mud shrimp at spots like Mary Point, Grand Anse, and Johnson's Mills. The peep fraternity, in order of importance to fidelity to the upper Bay, are the following  *sandpipers*: *semipalmated*, *white-rumped*, *least* (a similar species is called "stint" in the U.K.), *Baird's*, and *western*. Late in the fall, when the November snow flurries swirl, the *dunlin* arrives. A special treat any time in the season are *curlew* and *stilt sandpipers*.

The *semipalmated plover*, it's the one with the single black bar on the chest, has its own satellite flocks on the flats. Quite bullish, this little plover when coming against another will chase it around, or simply hop over its opponent. Something to see.

Two larger plovers: the *black-bellied* and the *golden* are in the area in fall. Preferred habitat for the golden are cow pastures and harvested hay fields, and sometimes golf courses.

Another gregarious member of the group is the wave-chasing *sanderling*. They usually stay in discrete flocks. The *red knot* (it's in non-breeding gray plumage when it visits us) and the *dowitchers* are among the larger of the group.

The pretty little *pectoral sandpiper* is found in small numbers on the fringes.

The eye-catching *buff-breasted sandpiper* with its striking white underwings is a rare visitor.

Large concentrations of any bird usually attract predators. In the case of the upper Bay of Fundy, *peregrines* and *merlins* make high tide passes over the beaches. They choose high tide as that's when the prey is concentrated at the head of the beach. Peripheral bird catchers are *northern harriers*, and both large *gulls* have a technique that often works. Both the herring and great black-backed gulls will mob a resting flock of small sandpipers attempting to crowd them into the water, rendering some of them so wet that they can't fly easily. *Red foxes* like shorebirds for lunch, too!

In the upper Bay of Fundy and also in the low profile shore of eastern New Brunswick, there are salt marsh pools and quiet lagoons. These places are the favoured resort of the super-active *greater* and *lesser yellowlegs*, *solitary sandpipers*, the *willet*, the *Hudsonian godwit* and flocks of *whimbrels*.

The whimbrels sometimes forage for crowberries on the dry bogs or for worms and insects in farm fields. Favoured places are the expanses of peat in Miscou, Shippagan and Lameque.

A rare nester throughout this Province, the *solitary sandpiper*, which favours a habitat of soggy bog ponds protected by clouds of black flies in warm weather, has a problem with a wet substrate. It gets around this nicely by commandeering the abandoned nests of shrub or bush nesting passerines of about its approximate build. Most likely choices are old nests of *robins*, *veerys*, *rusty*, and *red-winged blackbirds*.

Two open-country shorebirds have abandoned the shore at least for rearing a family. The familiar *killdeer* (plover) prefers sparsely vegetated gravel pits, airport runway aprons, and vacant lots. The graceful *upland sandpiper* nests sparingly west of Moncton. It desires large fields and open country.

New Brunswick's east coast is attractive to the endangered *piping plover*. The dunes of Kouchibouquac National Park and Buctouche Bar are safe havens for this delightful little plover. The resource staff of both the national park and the Irving Nature Park at the Bar take their stewardship seriously.

Both in appearance and habitat choice, the *common snipe* and *woodcock* are similar. In the fine tuning, though, the snipe prefers sedge meadows and marsh edges. For woodcock the presence of *alders* is important. Both use vibrating feathers as part of the spring courtship repertoire. The snipe makes a "winnowing" sound with specialized tail feathers as it descends to earth after flying to a height. The offering of the woodcock is a bit more elaborate, consisting of chippering, twittering sounds. It's also produced aerially, with modified outer primary feathers. This "sky dance" has many fans.

Brian Dalzell, working with the Fundy Bird Observatory on Grand Manan, has documented the recent summer appearance of a few *American oystercatchers*. By 2002 they had not been confirmed as nesting on any of several small islands off the main island of Grand Manan. It's where they had been seen, but probably just a matter of time. Good work, Brian!

 The *herring gull*, which personifies all the fine adaptations of this group, is the most widespread and numerous of its kind in N.B. It does everything well: walking, swimming and flying, and besides isn't diet restricted, eating just about anything.

The population of the larger, *great black-backed gull* is about 10% of that of the herring gull.

Looking like a trim version of the herring gull, the *ring-billed gull* is increasing steadily in our area.

In the last few years a small colony of the *black-legged kittiwake* has established a beachhead on the isolated Wolves. These are small islands off the shore of Charlotte County in the vicinity of Grand Manan.

If you've noticed large gulls that tend to be "whiter" in the winter time, you've spotted either the *glaucous* (the size of the great black-backed), or the *Iceland gull* (herring gull sized).

We have four *terns* that nest in N.B. The three black-capped, fork-tailed terns are the *Arctic, common* and *roseate.*

The Arctic has a large colony of several thousand on Machias or Seal Island south of Grand Manan. The cold turbulent waters simulate the much more usual environment for this tern further north. So, I guess we're lucky to have 'em.

Common terns have huge colonies, still, on the east coast along the Kent and Westmorland County shores.

Ever since gulls became protected in the early 1900's terns have had a struggle protecting themselves, their eggs and chicks from their marauding larger relatives.

One or two pairs of the beautiful roseate tern nest on Sea Island among the booming Arctic and common tern pairs on Seal Island off Grand Manan. (Nova Scotia shelters about a 100 pairs of roseates.) The black tern is a freshwater marsh inhabitant. It's quite local along the lower St. John in N.B., from just north of Fredericton south. New Brunswick harbours the only significant population of these swallow like terns in the Maritimes.

An icon of the Irving Nature park near Saint John and the Atlantic Coastal Action Program in the same city, the *great blue heron* stirs the imagination of most of us. It's a consummate fisherman. As it's shy and sometimes forages at night we don't always get to appreciate its skill directly. There are more than a dozen colonies of these long-legged, long-necked birds in N.B.

Our second most common heron, is the well named *black-crowned night heron.* It nests in small colonies in two widely separated areas here in New Brunswick, in the north in Madawaska County, and one of the islands off the main Grand Manan.

A third heron is the green-backed. It's a small, roughly crow-sized bird that stays in the cover around shady ponds and creeks. It's famous for baiting fish to within range of its dagger-like bill by dropping flower petals or other items foreign to the fish's environment.

The *great egret* and the *snowy egret* both nest well south of our region, but they sometimes visit us in their post-breeding season wandering. They could show up just about any August or September in coastal salt marshes; for example, Saint's Rest west of Saint John.

15. A Parade of Waterfowl and Friends

Swans are more like *geese* than geese are like *ducks*.

Both members of the pair in the swans and geese are visually similar, family duties are shared, and both members of the pair stay with the family.

In ducks looks are often quite different, and the weight of perpetuating the next generation falls to the female. This is a bit ironic as ducks have up to 10-12 young per season compared to 4 or 5 young geese or swans raised by two adults. The ratio of adult to inexperienced young is 1: 10 for ducks to a much lower one of 1: 2 or 3 for swans and geese. Empathy should be directed to a very busy and stressed mother duck.

Sex ratios support the plight of the female duck. In the larger swans and geese it's fairly close to 50:50. In all duck species, males outnumber females, and among the diving ducks, the male-female ratio is roughly 70:50. Obviously, the life expectancy of female ducks is less than the males of the same species.

Waterfowl mortality from two sources is skewed towards the female ducks. During the approximately one month incubation period, the female is vulnerable. And hunting mortality is preferential to the females, as they tend to fly in front (into the decoys) first.

Among many animals where mate guarding, territorial defense, and harem style breeding are prevalent, the male's span is much shorter than the female's. This is well demonstrated in both the *ruffed grouse* and the *white-tailed deer*.

Ducks may feed in areas a long way from water, and may nest up to a mile from water. All ducks, however, must have regular access to water in some form or other. Geese too have an affinity for water, but they are much better equipped for terrestrial life than ducks. Geese actually graze on grass, something few ducks do. The *American widgeon* is one dabbling duck that grazes often enough for this activity to be a regular part of its behavior. Swans, well equipped with a meter-long neck to find all their food while afloat, specialize in submerged aquatics. These plants are unavailable to all but a few dabblers, which are typically capable only of tipping up. An exception is the long necked *Northern pintail*, that can reach to fair depth. Diving ducks, however, are able to go to considerable depths to reach desirable foods. No known aquatic plants would naturally occur at a greater depth than they could dive to.

While we are not exactly Canada's DUCK FACTORY we do have some excellent pocket wetlands, sweet and salt marshes, fens, and many beaver dams which are good brood-rearing habitat. Not to be discounted are man-made farm ponds. For both spring and fall staging there are wide stretches of major rivers and a few big lakes, such as Grand Lake in the St. Croix watershed, Grand Lake south of Fredericton, South Oromocto Lake, Loch Alva, Lake Petitcodiac, Long Reach on the St. John, and Kennebecasis Bay. In spite of our comparative dearth of extensive habitat we do have a good range of breeding waterfowl and visits from many other species as vagrants from both the west and northern Europe.

No members of the swan tribe nest in New Brunswick although, pre-contact, the trumpeter nested as close as Ontario and New England.

 Canada geese have been transplanted to southern New Brunswick from Ontario. They have taken to the marshes and meadows as a goose to a grain field! This is their first nesting in this province for over a century. The *Canada's* that are birds of passage here in spring and fall are the mid-sized "canadensis" race.

A few other local populations are the "maxima," which as the name hints are the largest. The mean weight of the giant Canada's is 5.2 kg., which compares to the mean of 4.0 kg., for the "canadensis." The cackling goose, which is small and dark, about the size of a mallard, weighs in at about 1.5 kg. It nests in coastal Alaska.

The "canadensis" form is the type that has become quite a nuisance on the golf courses of southern New England and Delmarva. This is the goose that has taken the U.K., one marsh and cow pasture at a time. It's the same story here as in the old country, the welcome is wearing thin. Canada geese carrying on the tradition of non-stop success are now colonizing western Greenland. They're apparently unstoppable!

We're still a few seasons away from the situation in the 1800's in this part of the country, when enlisted men stationed here petitioned the authorities not to have to eat wild goose eggs any more than twice a week in the spring!

In the dim mists of past times, the *branta* geese, of which the Canada is a member, were sea geese, spending the bulk of their lives on or near the saltings. Corn and grain fields weren't in their visitation repertoire back then.

The small, actually dainty, brant (or brent) geese, nest on the coasts of the high Arctic, wintering in the tide zones of Cape Cod. A satellite flock of several thousand spends time in Grand Harbour on Grand Manan, arriving as early as February on the way north. The east coast of Grand Manan is now well supplied with marine eel grass, a brant favourite.

As for other geese, the beautiful *greater snow goose*, whose North American population is in a buoyant phase, spills over to us when either north or southbound. Its visits are increasing in frequency particularly to the border area between New Brunswick and Nova Scotia, but also to Saint's

Rest Marsh just west of Saint John. A few falls ago flocks of these striking birds appeared in widely separated areas of the province, including the Tobique valley.

The *white-fronted goose*, and the *barnacle goose* have both shown up in the southern portion of the province.

The *mallard* throughout the world is the "wild duck" of choice. It's quite a common nester and even a winter resident here. It wasn't always that way. However, releases and the modification of the environment making it resemble farm country further west (Ontario and the Prairies) made the "greenhead" quite at home.

We always did have our own "mallard," namely the so-called *black duck drake*. This forest mallard is actually a beautiful shade of brown. Admittedly, it does look dark, maybe black in the distance, especially under reduced light. In spring breeding finery the drake has a rich dark brown body, contrasting smartly with a straw coloured, brown-streaked head and neck. The mate is paler but similar in pattern, and both sexes have deep purple speculums at the inner bend of the wings.

The mallard speculum is ultramarine in colour and smartly edged with white borders. Quite striking, too, are the pure white underwing coverts.

Proof that these two species are very closely related is the high incidence of fertile crosses between them. It's theorized that the black duck arose as a separate species as a result of thousands of years of isolation. The black duck drake is a bit on the plain side. Without competition from other more natty species, it wasn't necessary to be spiffed up.

When the influx of mallards began in earnest there was a concern that these more colourful birds would put the black out of commission as a full species. When the push of releases was curtailed, the native black duck did a lot better.

In our little survey of ducks we can talk breeding plumages of drakes, body sizes, and species specific habits if any. In setting the ground rules, an elemental principal is that the diving ducks tend more towards contrasting black and white as set against the earth tones and greens and browns of the drake dabblers.

As to glamour in the paddling crowd, we have a few nominees. The *harlequin duck* is set off with areas of white and black against a deep blue body colour. It displays a rusty flank.

With rich greens, blues and deep wine colours the *wood duck* vies with the Asiatic mandarin for the title of most beautiful duck in the world. The harlequin has been confirmed as a very rare breeder in the Jacquet River in northeastern N.B. The wood duck, rare in the 1930's, is now a reasonably common nester in the lower St. John River system, west to St. Stephen, and east to Sackville, wherever duck boxes have been provided. It avoids coastal salt marshes. Of our three *merganser species*, the smallest of the tribe, the *hooded* is very eye-catching. Key to the classiness is the hood that is raised and lowered depending on the level of excitement of the owner at that time. While not the target, the "hoodie," benefits from the wood duck box program.

Contenders with the wood duck and others in beauty and appearance are four species of puddle ducks, or dabblers.

The *northern shoveller*'s plumage pattern reminds one of the mallard. Its large spoon-shaped bill gives the bird a somewhat droll appearance. It's a local nester in southern N.B.

The *northern pintail* has a chocolate brown head and neck and a beautiful long pointed tail. It's sometimes called the greyhound of the duck kingdom.

The *American wigeon*, formerly called the baldpate, is a striking bird with gray-pinkish flanks and a black rump set against white. An area of green extends around the eye and down the neck. Our native wigeon, which has expanded its population in the southern reaches since 1960, is an aggressive duck, even bravely floating among feeding Canada geese so as to grab any loose morsel that the larger birds don't quickly control.

Every once in a while a (*Eurasion*) *wigeon* will appear, often singly.

The fourth pretty duck is the drake *blue-winged teal*. Its trademark head pattern includes a facial cresent of white set against blue-grey. Its two sister species are the cinnamon teal of California, and the garganey of Europe and central Asia. There's at least one N.B. record for the garganey.

The *green-winged teal* and the diving *bufflehead* are the smallest dabbler and diver respectively. The little greenwing is a quick and perky duck. They seem to be constantly eating, leading to the comment that they should be among the birds to increase in size. It doesn't happen. The size may come into play in the utilization of nesting habitat, as the mother teal will raise her brood in a pool hardly bigger than a bathtub. The cavity-nesting bufflehead raises its family north and west of here.

Two *goldeneyes* are seen here. The *common* has a pure white flank and a round facial disk. With more black in the body, the *Barrow's goldeneye* has a half-moon crest on the front of its face. The common goldeneye is a common nester in nest boxes intended for woodies. It's often called the "whistler." An appropriate name, for even in early January the wintering flocks demonstrate a lot of courtship behavior. The bright white flanks against the black bodies of the drake goldeneye is certainly eye-catching in winter sun. Amorous, or confused, drakes vie for the attentions of the less numerous brown-headed and gray-bodied females by doing a stereotyped head throw accompanied by a very unducklike "beeeeep!" They're a little anxious, considering that goldeneyes, like most divers, are relatively late nesters. They're about a month after the black ducks and mallards, which can initiate the nest by late March.

Wintering sites are sheltered coves along the Bay of Fundy, especially from Saint John west. A popular brackish water site is at Harding's Point-Westfield about 12 km. up the St. John River from the harbour. Sometimes up to a thousand divers will congregate at this location, a mixed-species flock of mostly common goldeneyes, with a few Barrow's goldeneyes, a few dozen buffleheads, a contingent of greater scaup (bluebills), in the shallower water, a modest number of mallards and blacks, and in late winter a discrete flock of Canada geese.

The *ring-necked duck* has become a frequent nester in the Maritimes within the memory of our oldest waterfowlers. They don't normally over-winter with us. A bit smaller than both scaups, they seem a little introverted in mixed spring flocks. Their preferred summer brood area is a chamaedaphne-lined bog pond. With legs placed far back on the body, they often nest within a few feet of the water's edge, often on a floating mat of sphagnum.

The *greater scaup*, apparently realizing that cattle no longer were grazing on mile-long Grassy Island, began peaceful nesting there in almost the density of a gull colony in the 1980's. Since then the vegetation, especially bushes kept at bay by the cattle, have made the island less suitable and reduced nesting attempts.

Lesser scaup are rare nesters in New Brunswick.

The *tufted duck*, a dapper sister species of the ring-neck and a native of Europe, has been detected a few times around the province. Birders were thrilled when the "first" one was a mint-plumaged drake that spent the better part of the winter of 1995-96 in company with greater scaup and common goldeneyes at Marble Cove just above Saint John Harbour. Then for a few succeeding winters this same bird (or a look-alike) arrived. Once it came early enough to be tallied on the Saint John Christmas Count.

Most diving ducks, like the goldeneyes, don't turn down a meal of fish, but the mergansers, especially the two larger kinds (the common and the red-breasted) are fish specialists. The larger of these two is the common, which tends to be more tied to fresh water, especially clean, fast flowing streams. This duck is our largest-bodied duck inhabiting fresh water. (Its habitat puts it in the position to eat salmon parr which can be abundant.) As a result it's not exactly loved by fly fishermen on these same streams.

Sometimes a female is encountered along the natal river with an extremely large brood. They're not all hers by the way; she's just a good mom and demonstrates it with action! The merganser flock will sometimes co-op fish; that is, swim into shallow water in a line, herding their prey. Extremely hardy, this merganser will spend the winter as far upstream as open water permits.

The drake *red-breast* is natty with his wild looking crest, something the common doesn't have. With a green head, a white collar, and ruddy chest he is similar to the unrelated drake mallard. Red-breasts prefer tidal rivers and may resort to pure salt water. If you see a courting party in the spring, you're in for a treat, as there's much curtseying and bowing. The common merg just does a lot of splashing around.

The slim, sleek-hooded merganser is the smallest of the tribe, and it's found in summer on small waters, quiet narrow creeks, beaver ponds, and secluded timber-to-shore coves. While equipped to catch fish, it probably doesn't pass up large aquatic insects and the bigger tadpoles.

The largest in the genus, the *canvasback* (affectionately called "canny"), is a true prairie slough resident. It craves wild celery, something that the odd loners that come this far east don't get. Its smaller cousin, the *redhead*, which has a chestnut head like the canny, also has a black chest and a generally gray body. This duck has been reported nesting sparingly in the extensive marshes of the N.S. - N.B. border, Amherst Point, John Lusby and the Maccan areas.

Lethargic is an adjective that has been applied to our largest duck, the *common eider*. Granted, it does take things calmly! Disturbance, egg gathering and hunting nearly wiped these fine big ducks off the map in the early years of the 1900's.

Mother eiders have their own mode of protection against marauding *great black-back gulls*. The biological mother "enlists" the aid of her daughters from the previous nesting season, and also her female siblings. Particularly the "aunts" form a circle around the ducklings; it's given the descriptive label of "creche."

What happened on New River Island, New River Beach Provincial Park, gives cause for hope. In 1973, only 6 nests were located. By 2000 this had grown to around 350.

Coloured bottom up, the drake *eider* is white on top and black below.

In spring, mixed sex flocks of eiders are winging their way to the rich Arctic nesting grounds. These long lines sometimes have a smaller darker guest, with pastel wash of powder blue on the head. This is a real treat, the *king eider.*

A favourite winter haunt for eiders, including the "king," is off Indian Point, just east of St. Andrews.

On the wintering grounds, the *harlequin* tends to duplicate the tumultuous natal streams by living in the environs of storm-tossed, seaweed covered rocks, crashing surf, and rip currents.

Drakes of two species of duck have long, streaming tail feathers. The *northern pintail* and, yes, the *long-tailed duck*. In less sensitive times, this tan and black, very northern duck was called simply, the "old squaw." Actually, it's the drakes that do most of the talking! These ducks are vocal, even melodious, leading to them being labeled "hounds" by Newfoundland fishermen. Very successful in achieving a population in the millions, they feed almost exclusively on clams, periwinkles and commercial mussels, raising the hackles of aquaculture people.

Only one species of *scoter* has "black" in its name, yet the drakes in all three species, that are passage migrants on the Bay of Fundy, are largely formally attired! It's the *black scoter* that's the most numerous in the counts of the Pt. Lepreau Bird Observatory. The extent of the nesting grounds of this scoter, and to a degree its sister species is but poorly delineated. A flock of a few hundred, mostly drakes, has had a tradition of passing the summer on the Musquash River estuary, just west of Lorneville.

The black scoter is the most vocal of the three. Both while in flight and when resting on the water they utter a melodious whistling sound.

As it has two separate patches of white on the head, the *surf scoter* is identified by wildfowlers as the "skunk-head coot!" The *white-winged scoter* is the largest of the clan, and as with the others its diet is basically shellfish. It also eats sea lettuce and eel grass.

The little, low-swimming *ruddy duck* is a whimsical fellow. Its late development cycle puts it in a vulnerable situation come the hunting season. At all times the adults are extremely hesitant to fly and the immatures just can't.

Here in New Brunswick, and the rest of the Maritimes, the closest thing to a pelican is the *cormorant*. Our nesting species is the *double-crested*. In flight they look like crooked necked geese that fly a bit raggedly. In migration they sometimes form the famous "V" formation of geese; alternatively, long skeins. (Reminder, a skein is from ME; means a tangle or confusion.)

Single or small lines of cormorants moving along low over the water are a constant feature of the rivers of southern New Brunswick. When not flying or fishing, cormorants form vampire-like silhouettes while wing drying in the sun, using piers, bouys, or unoccupied boat decks for this resting time. To observe their considerable skill in fish capture, visit Reversing Falls Rapids during either dominant down tide or at the height of incoming tide. You'll not be long before you see a *gaspereau*, a *blue back herring*, even an *eel* being swallowed. *Herring gulls* are circling around ready to snatch a meal they didn't work for, and often harbour seals are bobbing their smooth, shiny heads in the sun.

The *common loon* approaches in size a small goose. One of our fascinating creatures, the "common" part of the name is not accurate, as this species, while widespread, wasn't ever truly commonplace. Even with the establishment of "Loon Police" and the provision of nesting rafts and other pro-loon measures, populations are in decline. Even having a cottage on a "loon lake" can have a negative effect. Subtle disturbance, attraction of nest-raiding raccoons, deterioration of water quality, lost monofilament fishing lines, and poisonous lead sinkers are all deadly. So enjoy those wild and crazy calls, yodels, and maniacal laughs. For the birds they're serious business, relating to the protection of mate and territory.

Another problem with *loons* is that they're not highly productive. Rarely do two chicks per nest survive. The parents favour the strongest chick. Consummate fishers, a pair of loons with a baby or two to nourish will take a tonne of fish out of a lake in one summer.

A bit smaller than the common loon, the *red-throated loon* nests well north of our area so it's on the Bay of Fundy in migration or in winter only. Flocks of around 50 frequent the shores of Cape Enrage on the upper Bay; otherwise they're at Point Lepreau and Musquash Harbour.

Grebes in some ways resemble loons physically, yet aren't closely related. Both groups with their feet well back are pro swimmers and divers but awkward on land.

Looking like a wet chicken, the *pied-billed grebe*,

has a bill like a barnyard fowl. It's the only grebe that regularly nests in N.B. Consistent with the life style, the nest is typically in the middle of a floating mat of decaying marsh vegetation and debris. The hatchlings are uniquely marked with dark stripes, reminding one of a feathered zebra. This grebe forages for food other than fish: shellfish, tadpoles, frogs, salamanders, leeches and large insects and spiders. For reasons that are best known to the grebe, these birds also ingest feathers with abandon, and even "feed" feathers to their offspring.

Secretive and skulking, it might be easier to hear the pied-billed grebe than to see it. At night eerie coos, whinnies or gobbling noises are offered. If the natal marsh has *rails*, you could be in for quite a concert.  Both the *horned* and *red-necked grebes* are uncommon winter visitors to our salt water. At this season they are out of breeding-season finery and practically attired in grays and whites.

"Being as thin as a rail" originally had reference to part of a fence structure, yet it fits well to a group of little known marsh dwellers. *Rails*, of which we have three species, can literally melt into the densest stand of bullrushes or cattails. At the last minute, if they're frightened into flushing out of their hideaway, their flight is weak and their route short. They look more like big-footed chickens than anything you'd expect to encounter in a wetland.

The *sora* (*rail*) is widespread, yet, as with the pied-billed grebe you'll be alerted to its presence by the descending whinny coming from deep in the marsh. It's related to the *corn crake* of the U.K. The *Virginia rail* is nearly as common as the sora here. They both have a centre of abundance in the N.B. - N.S. border marshes.

It is in this landscape of extensive marshes and meadows that the much rarer and super secretive *yellow rail* lurks. A small (vulnerable?) community of *yellow rails* was recently discovered in the Grand Lake meadows near Jemseg.

Like grebes, the *coot* is lob-footed rather than web footed. The coot and the *moorhen* swim with a jerky neck action as would a chicken walking on land.

Nesting of the (common?) moorhen, which is a rare and local occurrence in the "Border Area," seems contingent on new artifical impoundments being in the full flush of a new vegetation stage. Most of these have been established by Ducks Unlimited Canada.

The *coot*, a chicken-billed "duck-wanna-be" reaches its greatest abundance in the same region, yet isn't quite so picky about habitat. Coots are quite gregarious by nature and form highly visible, noisy, active flocks, which is in contrast to their cousins the *skulky rails*.

Focusing on a vegetable diet coots will also consume a wide variety of invertebrates: crayfish, prawns, snails. They also eat small fish and tadpoles, and have been caught savouring other birds' eggs!

To get up close and friendly with ducks and other denizens of the marsh, take the boardwalk around Sackville

Waterfowl Park. Mallards and muskrats aplenty.

If you enjoy watching the antics of mothers and their ducklings, from early to mid-summer flotillas of various species are in evidence. Most families are mallards, with a fair contingent of *blacks, wigeon, green-winged teal*, and from the divers, the *ring-necked duck.*

The Park is a fine spot to see *pied-billed grebe* families; those zebra-striped youngsters often ride on Mom's back.

Kingfishers and *tree swallows* often are seen flying over the marsh.

As to long-legged waders, the good old "blue crane," more correctly the *great blue heron* is a visitor. The *bittern* is around. And *skulky rails* do their turn through the cattails. If you don't see the *sora* or the *Virgina rail*, you may hear their maniacal utterances.

From mid-August on, both *greater* and *lesser yellowlegs* loaf on mud bars in the marsh between tide cycles.

The Sackville Waterfowl Park is well worth a visit, and as a bonus, there's an excellent waterfowl-wetlands display in the nearby Canadian Wildlife Service building.

16. Intermission: Clowns and Comedians

Perhaps a bit unfairly, some animals are considered amusing. Among the birds and mammals the following have been selected: the *raven*, the *blue jay*, the *ruffed grouse*, the *woodcock*, the *kingfisher*, the *common loon*, the *moose*, the *otter*, the *red fox*, *grey* and *red squirrels*, the *black bear* and the *porcupine*.

Generally serious, the raven does seem to have fun.

During courtship these birds show exuberance. When a pair, or several pairs, on a bright February morning are doing barrel rolls, loop the loops, or even somersaults high over the valley, even the most sober of us has to smile. *Ravens* have been spotted doing an otter-like imitation of sliding on snow. Any slight incline will do. As they reach the highest elevation, they flip over on their backs and slide down! Then they'll either walk or fly back to the top. A pair of *ravens* can easily steal a sleigh dog's dinner. Co-operating, the first raven pulls the dog's tail while the second rushes in to grab the food, or even pull the dish beyond the dog's reach, which works well if the victim is tied.

Another comic is the *blue jay*. They're real teases. They steal nuts that *squirrels* have cached and fly away to some secluded hiding place. Masters of imitation, they'll use this skill to their benefit. A hawk-like scream will often free up a source of food. Jays, devils in blue, are extremely secretive around their own nests, but otherwise noisy, frightening other birds in to revealing their nests so they can filch an egg or two.

Certainly it's not deliberate, but the drumming of the *ruffed grouse* rooster is a cause of amusement. Imagine beating your wings (or arms) against the air to make a thumping sound to attract members of the opposite sex? Seems to us humans to be a lot of work. Investigators have found that it uses significant energy in the form of calories burnt. First Nation parents explained the sounds coming from the spring woods as Glooscap, their God and leader, building a giant canoe!

Not only does he look amusing, the *woodcock* has a

few anatomical features that can turn heads: an extremely long bill coupled with ridiculously short legs and eyes on the back of his head. Quite a combo, but it works. The placement of the eyes is an adaptation for watching for predators while the bill is deep in the ground extracting juicy earthworms. Short, sturdy legs are best when you're in a tangled habitat such as an alder bed, preferred by the *woodcock*. We're not finished with this fellow yet. To many, to hear a male woodcock, or duelling male woodcocks deliver their aerial courtship in a spring dusk is a very satisfying emotional experience. A mix of oral and mechanical sounds produces a unique effect enhanced by its delivery, which commences high above the earth's surface. Part of the sound display is produced by vibrating outer wing feathers. No wonder it's called a "sky dance."

Just about everything about the belted *kingfisher* is odd, no offence meant. Think about it. Here we have a *woodpecker* relative that dives head first into a pond or stream to catch minnows. It nests in a cavity like its kin, yet instead of a nice dry tree hole, it burrows into a streamside bank. Also, that loud rattling call could hardly be something to be proud of. And what about that unruly topknot! Sorry, kingfisher.

"Crazy as a loon" is a comment that's not fashionable nowadays in reference to the icon of northern lakes, the *common loon*. So if that eerie yodeling call does sound weird, it's still beautiful.

According to one legend passed down by the First Nations People (who also named this majestic animal), the *moose*, funny looking fellow that he is, was made from leftovers in Glooscap's shop. No one wanted that long nose, those gangly legs on too short a body, that excuse for a tail. And that bell, an afterthought.

In reality, the anatomy of "Bullwinkle" is the result of eons of adaptation and modification to the environment. Consider the value of long strong legs in going through an oozing swamp in summer, or snow banks to your arm pits in winter. Why would any animal need a long neck, when most of the browsing is done at eye level? In winter, browsing on *fir*, the moose winter food, is super efficient with that flexible muzzle, the equivalent of a big Christmas tree can be converted to moose food in about 15 minutes, about the time most of us take over our coffee. Some might shake their heads at the bell, but it too has a distinct purpose. During the rut when the bull rolls in his wallow, which is perfumed with his urine, the bell is effective as a scent dispenser.

Maybe the raven got the idea of sliding downhill from that incurable slider, the *river otter*. Otters, whole families of them, seem to slide strictly for fun. A well-used slide, usually established on a moist slope ending in water, will have the appearance of an Olympic bob sled run. The otter's slide is usually near the family's den, or "holt."

Red foxes put that beautiful white-tipped tail to effective use in luring curious ducks to close range. It's pure ruse, using a number of elements including the natural inquisitiveness of waterfowl, the bushy cover usually present at waterside, and the skillful ballet of a fox running back and forth while partly screened. A duck's eye view is only of the dancing white-tipped tail. The popular Nova Scotia Duck Tolling Retriever capitalizes on this trait of ducks; the dog behaves like a fox. The *coyote*, however, related to both characters and described as a "trickster", is not equipped for tolling.

Maybe the antics of *grey* and *red squirrels* are more mischievous than humorous. As to those "squirrel proof" feeders, so called, generally the squirrel wins! Squirrels have their way with the feathered competition.

A lady living in Quispamsis, who enjoys squirrels, once placed food at the mouth of one of their snow burrows. A few minutes later, returning to the comfort of her living room, she looked out to see one of the squirrel family busily covering up the treasure with snow, while keeping an eye on some very interested jays.

The *woodchuck* gains a bit of celebrity by its spot on the calendar: "Ground Hog Day." Technically, it's a ground squirrel.

It's a bit pathetic how we have characterized the black bear, once, and perhaps still, a totem animal to some groups of our First Nations People. At times bears appear shambling, awkward and a bit clumsy. Don't be fooled. They're not only strong but quick and precise if they need to be. An Albert County farmer once showed me the carcass of a porcupine that had been completely eviscerated by a bear, a neat technical job. And, as far as that winter down time is concerned, who doesn't admire an animal that not only doesn't go about in blizzards but who likely doesn't even hear them howling!

The *porcupine* is a prickly fellow, and while he may

not be a good option as a cushion, he is in his own way a bit amusing. Imagine a craving for salt so strong that you'd chew a privy seat. Porcupines do it.

And when courting in the late summer, they are programmed to hug. They have even been observed hugging stumps.

Throwing quills isn't one of their skills, though the smartly slapped tail in the direction of their enemy, real or perceived, gives that impression. A smart dog won't get stuck twice!

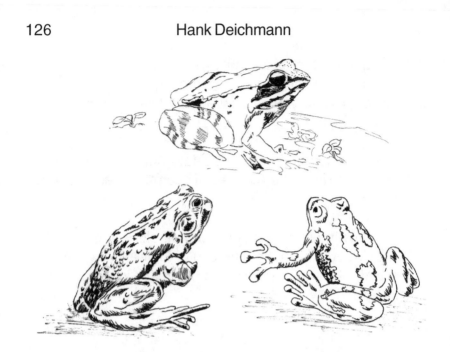

17. These Aren't Foul and Loathsome Creatures

It's a sunny afternoon, pleasantly warm for mid-April. We're in a rough pasture with scattered flat stones and a few bleached, rotting stumps. We're on a south-facing slope near Kars on the Belleisle. There is no snow left here, though there may well be some in the shade of the nearby woods. A small stream in the middle of the pasture leads down to a creek. It's flowing strongly, yet it's not overflowing.

We lift together a heavy stump. Underneath some *carab beetles* go scurrying, a couple of *earthworms* slide out of sight.

While Mark investigates a rotting log, I turn over a medium-sized flat chunk of *sandstone*. I'm surprised to see something beautiful, a tightly coiled *garter snake*. It's groggy and only slowly lifts its head to regard the disturber. It's attired in shades of brown in long stripes, therefore the name. I estimate its length to be about three feet, mature but not a record. Mark comes over to look and then we carefully place the rock roof back over this wonderful animal.

The garter snake is by far the largest snake native to this Province. It's also the most widespread and commonest. It is more than twice the length of any of the other three snakes. The garter will only offer to bite if it's made upset and nervous. None of our snakes are poisonous. None are foul or loathsome.

Some "garters" are golden brown, a local colour phase, hinting at the range possible in this adaptable species. Garter snakes bear living young. A typical group of newly born garter snakes will number about 30, each about six inches long, and varying greatly in colour and patter; each one is an individual.

The next largest is the *ring-necked snake* that can reach a modest 20 inches in length. This snake has a yellow ventral surface and a pale buff ring around the neck.

Mark mentions that he has found creatures hiding in a wet rotting log. When we investigate further, I confirm that these are non-aquatic *salamanders*. They're small, less than five inches long, and sepia in colour matching the hues of the pine wood where they are living. These are the *red-backed salamanders*. Unless they move they're difficult to see. With low-slung bodies and short legs, they look a bit like *lizards* to which they are not at all related. Think about it, these animals prefer dark and damp; lizards like heat and dry. These salamanders lay eggs in small clusters in the cavities of their home log. The salamander clan eats small insects and earthworms.

Moving across the slope, we find more stones to roll over. The third one is lucky. Here are several, actually four, *red-bellied snakes*, docile and loosely coiled. One of their number obligingly turns over, showing its red belly. They're adult, yet all are under 10 inches in length. Three of them have two light spots at the back of the head, and it's easy to see how one might confuse them at first glance with the similar sized ring-necked snake. Not as often found as the much larger garter snake, the red-bellied is common and widespread. Like the garter snake it bears live young, with up to 20 two to three inch young, being born at a time.

Elated by our luck we carry on with this crazy activity of stone turning. We know we're obsessed. We wonder what any spectators would think? Fortunately, the countryside is too busy to bother with rock turners. By now we've lost count of the number of "turnings." Then Mark calls out, "Look at what I found!" I walk over, and there is a very large and grouchy toad. If it was smaller, it could be a potential snake dinner. As we did with the others we put back his, or her, roof too.

We didn't find any smooth *green snakes*, they emerge later in the spring when the temperatures are higher than mid-April. The "green" is our smallest snake, and in the summer greenery they are very difficult to detect. This snake and the ring-neck both reproduce by laying eggs.

After a sandwich and beverage break and a stretch out in the late afternoon sun, we're charged to go again. Downslope this time, we're headed for the creek. Crossing a water-filled ditch we see moving brown forms about the length of a legal trout, but when we look more closely, the round yellow spots on these creatures are a clincher for the *spotted salamander*, the largest we have. These run about eight inches long.

This spotted salamander will be readily visible for only a week or so. After the eggs are laid they will seclude themselves, mole-like, well under the surface and out of our sight until the rains of the next spring tempt them out again. So feast your eyes!

Off the slope we now find ourselves in an open floodplain forest. Our passage through the dry leaves of the silver maples and ashes is uncomfortably noisy. We can hardly hear the thin songs of the *yellow-rumped warblers* high above us. Fortunately, we pause; otherwise we would have missed a plodding *turtle* with a red neck and red legs. Sometimes called "old red legs," the *wood turtle* has a highly sculptured shell. He's a quiet fellow, peaceable as indicated by his diet of worms and beetles, snails, slugs, minnows, tadpoles and strawberries.

This specimen crosses our path at right angles, very purposefully, hinting at an intimate knowledge of a home range.

The *wood turtle* is less than a foot long, dwarfed by

the *snapper*, largest of New Brunswick's inland turtles. It can go to three feet in total length. It has a big head and a hooked jaw. We saw a large female intent on laying eggs on a sandbar in a previous spring, on Den Brook up in Queens County. Needless to say, that time we cut short our fishing trip!

In our collective dim past, intrepid First Nations people would seek out *snapping turtle* eggs by probing sandy banks with flexible twigs to find caches of eggs. A white boy, John Giles, a one-time captive of the Maliseets, reported their fondness for turtle eggs. John, who was eventually released unharmed to European settlers around 1650, kindly left us a written description of his experiences.

The *painted turtle*, with a smooth carapace of up to seven inches, is our smallest turtle. It's also the most colourful. The carapace is brown with red and black designs. There are round yellow markings on the head, and its belly (ventral surface) is yellow. Quite local in distribution, it's most common around Grand, Sunpoke, and Magaguadavic Lakes.

 As dusk is falling, finally we reach the edge of a quiet backwater pond. High above us a *woodcock* is doing his musical sky dance. In the vastness of the marsh beyond we're aware of the thunder-pump courtship call of the secretive *bittern*. We soon forget the distant bittern, though, when we hear a very high-pitched, chirping call. Soon a chorus of hundreds are "singing." We're being treated to a mating aggregation of spring *peepers*, our smallest and loudest *frog*! This deafening symphony almost drowns out the rattling snores of the *leopard frog* and the sporadic offering of our second largest in the clan, the "banjo plucking" *green frog*. The giant of the lot, the *bullfrog*, isn't active this early in the spring. A confirmed bully, the bullfrog will not turn down another frog as a meal, or even a small garter snake, not to mention meadow voles or any injured bird. In between, it satisfies its appetite with *dragonfly* larvae, *tadpoles*, *beetles* and even *butterflies* that come too close.

Slightly larger than its close relative the spring peeper, the *grey tree frog* has quite a different call, a long resonating trill. It's best appreciated in Hyla Park, set up for it's protection, in the southern outskirts of Fredericton.

The *woodcock* is still romanticizing when we break out our flashlights for the trek back to our transportation. We pledge a trip back to the rough pasture in mid summer to check out nests of garters and the other snake babies.

18. Creepy Characters

Here in New Brunswick we're fortunate to have a fine array of mammals, say about 35 species, and birds, about 350 different kinds. But insects and their associates, arthropods and some miscellaneous groups, number literally thousands.

Maybe I can credit my rural birth, but I can't remember ever being horrified by insects and other creepy crawlies. And now I understand that our youngest grandson, presently living in Norway, is a bugman in waiting.

So many well known groups to choose from: *ants*,

bees, beetles, flies, dragonflies, moths and *butterflies.* And there's *spiders,* which are eight-legged *arthropods,* having one set more than the insect format.

 There's so much to see, and unbelievably, if you look closely, you can enjoy these animals at all seasons of the year. *Spiders,* in particular, I even meet in winter, sometimes when doing a simple task like bringing in wood, or out snowshoeing, cross-country skiing, and snowmachining. True, at this season, they do move deliberately, even slowly. Still they must have great antifreeze. We know that even on the coldest winter day a dark coloured door in full sun will be well above freezing. The same applies to the dark trunks of trees. Just under the surface in these protected micro-environments *carpenter ants, wood borers,* and *beetles* live out their span, and are often active through the winter.

Insects and *arthropods* at various life stages, often at the larval stage, are the main source of protein for many young birds, from *grouse* chicks and *ducklings,* to baby *sparrows, warblers* and *flycatchers.* There's a good biological rationale for this: proteins are the building blocks for young bodies. As those young bodies mature, in some groups they change over to seeds, carbohydrates, fruits and berries, which come down to sucrose, or glucose, i.e., simple sugars.

We owe a great debt to most insects for their role in the food chain. Some mammals eat much protein from arthropods: the *shrews,* the *bats,* and in the case of some species at some seasons, *mice* and *voles.* Some of the larger mammals are surprisingly dependent on insects. *Skunks* spend a lot of time digging out grubs. And what about *bears* and their affection for *ants*? And their secondary consumption of *bees* when they bravely raid a bee hive.

A number of insects are noxious and infamous. Most folks are turned off by *earwigs* and *cutworms*. And anyone that's seen the damage caused by *forest tent caterpillars, gypsy moths,* or the *spruce budworm* is left in awe, and maybe in disgust.

On a more positive note most insect lives, granted they are intense, are fascinating. Ever see a mating pair of dragonflies flying along coupled? Or witness a migration of monarch butterflies along a windy coastline? Or show a youngster the workings of a golden-rod gall insect? Or experience a swarm of Mayflies that have been developing for months but only live for 24 hours when adult? The next morning there'll be a major windrow of their bodies on the beach.

Fireflies have an interesting story; both males and females flash as part of the courtship. (Fireflies are actually beetles.) The males do the more obvious flash as they deliver their signal from the air. Females signal from a ground location. Each species has a sort of morse code, or a signature, to the presentation of the flashes. Each species has a preferred space of time to carry out the signaling, so the time of the peak of the flashing is specific for each species. In a bizarre twist the females of the larger kinds sometimes signal to attract males of smaller species, and thereby capture and eat them!

What follows is a quick review of some interesting aspects of insect lives.

On/In the Water:
On the water we find *water striders*. These are the "bugs" (Hemiptera) that seem to skate over the surface of a pool or a backwater of a brook.

As the name suggests, back swimmers move about upside down!

Whirligig beetles are sociable, travelling in large packs, and fast (whirling) too. Whirligigs have divided eyes permitting them to see in air and through water simultaneously.

Predaceous diving beetles are an awesome predator, being the size of the bowl of a soup spoon.

 Sometimes called the "eagles of the insect world," dragonflies are of particular interest and quite visible. We're well above 30 different dragon flies in New Brunswick. We have quite a few different kinds of damsel flies too.

In the Fields of Summer:
In the fields of summer, *crickets* and their close relatives, *grasshoppers*, abound. In the cool summer evenings we enjoy the strident calls of the cricket.

Earlier in the summer, the almost round, walnut-sized June beetles (bugs) go blundering into screen doors. Like bumble bees they shouldn't be able to fly! Yet they do!

On Summer Evenings:

Lepidopteras, the *moths* and *butterflies* are among the most eye-catching of insects. (There's a field guide that aids the naturalist in watching these insects with binoculars.) Then at the other end of the life cycle, cocoons can be collected for the purpose of seeing what emerges. If searching for cocoons is too much trouble, caterpillars can be reared to pupation with the same result.

Social insects, *colonial ants* and *bees*, are fun to watch. The intricacies of their lives and how individuals relate to one another is in itself a fascinating study. Maybe even meaningful for humans.

19. Squirrels that Glide,
Mice that Fly, other Mice,
Sparrows that Run!

You're right, *flying squirrels* can't fly, but they are expert gliders.

Even where common, they aren't often seen, as they are nocturnal. Preferred habitats are tall mature hardwoods and softwoods, in hill country, cut up with ravines. In the evening as dusk falls, the flying squirrel contingent leave their daytime resting places in old woodpecker nests and hollow trees, climb to the highest branches, and prepare to launch themselves. The higher the launch pad the better, with 60 feet above the ground being a popular height. They glide at about a 45 degree angle, moving quickly, steering mostly with the wide tail and by adjusting the flaps of skin between the fore and hind legs. Just before making a landing, it's heads up with hind feet making contact first. The landing site is often a tree trunk.

A flight of 30 meters isn't at all unusual; 50 is up near the observed maximum. If our little aviator then remains motionless, he will be very hard to discern, as the monochrome gray pelage makes an excellent match for most lichen-encrusted, furrowed bark of *red spruce, maples, ashes* and other hardwoods.

The beautiful soft-furred squirrel of the night, in part as a reflection of its mobility, has a greater variety of food sources available to it, and finds them quicker too than its daytime relatives, the *red* and *gray squirrels*.

Within its home territory of several hectares the flier will key in on tree blossoms in May, and through the summer, seeds, fruit and nuts. In between there are ripe mushrooms and other fungi to sample, and the little flier isn't going to turn down a nest of bird's eggs, nestlings, or a deep sleeping parent!

While the flier is performing covert activities under the cover of darkness, it is vulnerable to *owls*

and *martens*. Spending a minimum of time on the ground, the *flying squirrel* isn't normally part of the diet of *foxes* and *coyotes* – or day flying *hawks* for that matter.

A literal translation of the German name for the bat is "flying mouse." Yes, they do fly, but they are definitely not mice. "Blind as a bat" is also erroneous. All our native bats see quite well and have the added advantage of precise echo-location, which is an efficient way to capture small, fast-flying insects.

Of eight species of bats possible in New Brunswick, by far the most commonly observed flying around at dusk, or taking up residence in the attic, are the little *brown bats*. If your home is of the vintage type and not 100% sealed, you may have to accept the little visitors; otherwise good construction techniques should discourage any invasion. If you want to reward them, put out a specific bat house, and you'll be rewarded with occupancy.

Other small bats are the *myotis*, the *pipistrelle*, and the *long-eared bat*, all three local and rare. Four larger species are all solitary, and, here, in the northern part of their migratory ranges. They are the *silver-haired*, the *red*, the *hoary* and the *big brown*. Sometimes they roost in trees. To spot one of these larger bats flying swiftly and strongly in the dusk is a great thrill for the naturalist.

True to its name, the *deer mouse*, although destructive around the closed up summer camp, is a truly beautiful little animal and does resemble its namesake in a number of ways. Its big eyes and ears are two features. The bi-colour pattern of warm brown above, contrasting with white below, is deer like. It's also very agile and moves gracefully, also like the deer we know so well. It is a rodent, as are the *voles* and *lemmings*.

Not as glamorous as the *deer mouse* are the *voles*. Both the *meadow vole/mouse* and the *red-backed vole* are common in the fields and conifer forests of New Brunswick. *Meadow voles* fashion runways, especially obvious after the snow melts in the spring.

Both *voles* are fecund. The *meadow vole* is strongly cyclic. I've found nests of baby *meadow voles* in early December when we had snow on the ground!

Another member of the group is the yellow-nosed *rock vole*. It does live among the rocks, being most frequent in northern parts of the province. Mount Carleton is a typical region.

It may come as a surprise to many that we have two species of *bog lemmings* in N.B. The *southern bog lemming* is the most widely distributed; the *northern* is most likely to be encountered in the northern part of the province. Both kinds are rounded in body shape, looking like small *meadow voles*. They do live in bogs.

Vying with the *deer mouse* for the prize of being good looking are the two species of *jumping mice*. With huge hind legs, they look like miniature kangaroos. As the names hint, the *meadow jumping mouse* prefers wet meadows, and the *woodland jumping mouse* sticks to forested stream banks. Both species are profound hibernators, sleeping for over half the year. They typically enter this state by mid-September.

Shrews look superficially like mice yet have very pointy noses and don't eat seeds or chew grass. Their fare is higher protein: insects, sow bugs, centipedes, earthworms, and even young mice.

Hyper is an understatement for all our native seven or eight species of *shrews*. For a *shrew* to see its first birthday is nothing short of a miracle. Mom shrews put on quite a spectacle when they take their family of up to 11 for a walk. Baby *shrews* follow one behind the other like a train. *Shrews* follow paths through the litter on the forest floor, and in the runs of larger mice they do a rodent run.

Moles, which are somewhat related to *shrews*, don't appear hyper at all. They burrow slowly and deliberately under the sod munching on *earthworms* and *grubs*. We only have one regularly occurring *mole*, the *star-nosed*, and if you see one that for some reason has emerged from the subterrean depths, you shake you head at those 22 tentacles around the nose and the wide hairy "hands" that look like they don't have arms. They look like awesome digging machines, which they are. *Moles* leave evidence of their works on the surface, ridges under which are their runways. Mole hills or mole castles are concentrations of excavated material.

Sparrows are a bit like feathered *mice*. They're brown, or beigy, streaked – in other words, well camouflaged. Like little rodents, they are efficient at seeking out weed and grass seeds. If startled, like frightened mice they do a "rodent run."

Birdwatchers call this group (and other difficult to identify birds) L.B.J.'s or Little Brown Jobs.

Savannah sparrows, quite simply, live on the savannah. Washed out streaky brown, they match the dry vegetation of windswept dunes, hayfields, and pastures. They are the ultimate "grass sparrow." Out in the tide-flooded salt meadows, the role of the *savannah sparrow* is taken over by the *Nelson sharp-tailed sparrow*. Both these *sparrows* have thin wheezy songs that seem to be carried away on the breeze.

The *song sparrow*, a beautiful singer, has this fact confirmed by the melodia part of its scientific name. Young male *song sparrows* in their first year listen carefully to the songs delivered by their fathers, and learn to imitate them. They refine their own song version with practise and by listening to neighbouring males, or Dad's competition!

A cousin of this sparrow is the *Lincoln's sparrow*. It's an expert skulker, very difficult to get in the clear for a good view. It makes use of wet bushy environments, and from concealment issues its complex structured song.

The *swamp sparrow*, another cousin of the *song sparrow*, does a repetitive song much like that of a *dark-eyed junco* or a *chipping sparrow*. Rather than swamps, they prefer tall rank marsh vegetation. Their nests are expertly concealed under a roof-like sheath of dry grass.

Dark-eyed juncos in slate-charcoal tones, have a colour pattern at odds with the rest of sparrowdom. Our friends to the south have a habit of terming them "snowbirds," as they appear with the first significant snow events, and reach further south than even the most intrepid *snow bunting*. Immature *juncos* are streaked brown, hinting that the true origin of these birds is indeed the *sparrow* clan!

It's possible that the white outer tail feathers of the adult junco are a predator foil.

Juncos are adept at working among trees, especially conifers. It's possible they gain some food items there.

The *tree sparrow* is more of a brushland sparrow, for it nests in Labrador-Ungava, and prefers weedy fields when it visits us in the south. It has a rusty cap as does the *chipping sparrow*, which summers with us in the Maritmes.

Hardy like the *tree sparrow*, the *fox sparrow* summers mainly to the north of New Brunswick. It's a robust, strong sparrow, our largest. The form we have is a "red" race, and the most colourful of the lot right across North America. Some of the larger *sparrows*, the *fox* among them, have perfected the double scratch – a headlong plunge while kicking backwards – great for stirring up leaves and litter and revealing insects and other "goodies."

The somewhat smaller *white-throated sparrow* does the double scratch and is a bird of striking plumage as well. It also has a pleasing song of clear whistles. This is translated by some as; "Sweet Canada, Canada, Canada........"

20. That Old Predator-Prey Cycle

What we're going to talk about here for the most part are *cats* and *dogs* and their relationship to a single *bunny*. The *cats*, two in number, are the *Canada lynx* and its southern cousin the *bobcat*, or as it's sometimes called, the "*bay lynx*." As for the *dogs*, they're also two in number. They're the *coyote*, a new boy on the block, and the *red fox*, which in its present form isn't quite what you might think! As for the "*bunny*," it's not even a *rabbit*. It's the wonderfully adapted *snowshoe hare*. Its alternate name is the *varying hare* which is also a good descriptive handle as, like the *ermine* and *ptarmigan*, this animal changes colour to suit the season. In some recent years the poor old hare has been out of sync, turning white too early, when there's no snow, and brown in the spring, when snow still lingers. For now we'll blame climatic warming.

Of the predators mentioned, it's only the *Canada lynx* that prospers or falters noticeably according to the numbers of the *hare*. So predictable are the peaks and valleys of the numbers of the predator and the prey that the cycle can be with confidence called the 10 YEAR cycle. That part of it is easy. It's the driving force that is the engine of the cycle that's a mystery. One of the most supported theories is that it's driven by food and its availability interacting with predator pressure. We're talking about browse material for the *hare* in this instance.

Before we get into numbers on the ground, let's talk about annual productivity. It's easy to see how the *hare* can sustain a fairly heavy pressure from the *lynx*. If a female (doe) *hare* has a moderate number of litters, say three per season, with say five young per litter, that's fifteen in one summer. The female *lynx* typically has from one to five kittens per year, the mean being three. At the top of a peak there may be a thousand *hares* per square mile, and at the bottom this could drop to twenty-five, or a ratio of 40:1. At the 25 number per square mile, we'll have some pretty thin, even gaunt *lynx*.

Bobcats which, like the *white-tail deer*, have moved north in quite recent times, are a lot more successful than the *lynx*. If it was possible to see them side by side, the long-legged big-footed *lynx* would seem larger than the more compact and small-footed *bobcat*. This is an illusion, as *bobcats* average heavier than the *lynx*. They are diet generalists, eating everything from *mice* to *deer*. They like *hares* but don't restrict themselves to them, as does the *lynx*, only hunting them in relation to their abundance and ease of capture.

Our *red fox* is a mouser, and its skill in this area has earned it the title "the most cat-like canid." It has a "mouse leap"; with unerring accuracy it can pounce on a victim up to five meters from the take-off point. *Foxes* chase *hares*, and *grouse*, and *pheasants*, too. Our native *foxes*, because of escaped fur-farm animals that were imported from England are now larger in stature than the founding population. This may have negative ramifications for the prey.

The *coyote* is the most recent addition to our New Brunswick roster of predators. It's incredibly adaptable and a survivor par excellence. It can hunt singly, if the prey is small, as is the *mouse*, or it can form packs when chasing down a *deer* on the frozen surface of a lake. As the subspecies of *coyotes* go, ours are among the largest. They are a pretty fair ecological fit for our former native *wolf*, which was small as *wolves* go. *Coyotes* won't turn down a meal of *hare*, especially if it's easy to obtain.

Other mammals that often include the *hare* in their dinner menu are *pine martens*, *fishers*, and the *mink*, which really prefers muskrats for its protein. Of the avian predators, the *goshawk* in the daylight and the *great horned owl* after dark would be taken seriously by any smart *hare*.

Even with all this "attention," the *hare* keeps hopping. It's the most expert of our snow travelers in the bush.

21. A Bunch of Rascals

The *mink* family is a big one here in New Brunswick, with seven present members. At least one additional member is extinct, and possibly another, the *wolverine*, may have wandered into our area occasionally. Not confirmed in this province, there's an old report from Nova Scotia. So a possible total of nine. All members run on land like a *seal* would if it had legs! Their bodies are relatively long and the legs are short.

The *mink* <u>Mustela</u> <u>vision</u> is a good standard representative of the family. It's about in the mid-range lengthwise, at about 60 cm. Compare it to the *otter*, at a 110 cm., at the high end, and the *ermine* at 20cm. at the bottom. As to life style it bridges the gap between an aquatic existence and the terrestrial. Hardly competition for the *beaver*, it's able to swim underwater for up to 100 feet, versus about half a mile for the *beaver*. This is still good enough to catch the odd *trout* or its favourite prey, the *muskrat*. *Mink* do all this, and as yet haven't developed webbed feet.

The regular *mink's* closest relative is now gone. The *sea mink* was once a resident of the coasts of northeastern New England; the Bay of Fundy, both New Brunswick and Nova Scotia sides; and the southwestern end of Nova Scotia. It was larger and more reddish in colour than the usually quite black standard *mink*. Sadly, the last of its kind was probably gone by the beginning of World War One. The last confirmed for New Brunswick was one taken in 1894 from Campobello Island.

Shaped like the smaller *ermine*, the *long-tailed weasel* almost reaches the length of a *mink*. It likes to hunt along streams, and is quite local in southern New Brunswick. The *ermine*, the smallest of the group, is the only one that changes colour with the seasons. I've seen them fully white by early November. Bloodthirsty for their size, they take down a wide variety of prey, up to young *hares*, or even farmyard *chickens*!

Martens are at home in trees, mostly to capture young birds. They are

reputed to be able to readily capture *squirrels*, but this is a rare event unless the *squirrel* is on the ground or really careless. In a chase through limber branches of *spruce*, the *red squirrel*, at an average of 200 gm., is considerably more agile than the *marten* that will average about four times as heavy. The real meat and potatoes for *martens* are the red-backed *voles*, the "moss mouse." They find them on the forest floor among the litter and what professional forest-wildlife managers call C.W.D., an acronym for coarse woody debris. There's lots of drama played out in these dark and shadowy places.

The *fisher*, the size of small *dog*, is a sort of overgrown *marten*. As it is black and sleek and moves really fast, it's responsible for a high percentage of "black cougar" sightings. Black *cougars* are folk lore; they don't really exist.

The *fisher* is mis-named, or at least the name is confusing, as, although it drinks water, it doesn't normally include *fish* in its diet. Its prowess is in catching *porcupines*, which makes it the lumberman's friend. It does its "quill hog" predation best in winter, when after biting the unprotected face of the porky, it burrows underneath, or flips it so as to gain access to the unprotected belly. I've been told by field biologists trapping *fishers* for transplanting that they are as surly and irritable as the *marten* is docile.

 *Otters* are a little like the *canaries* in coal mines; they are sensitive to pollution, as are their prey, *fish*. It seems *otters* are able to catch whatever *fish* are available in their home waters: *trout*, *perch, pickerel* and *bass*. They also eat *crayfish*, *frogs* and *turtles*. The home of the *otter*, a den in a

stream or river bank, is called a holt. Nearby there'll be a bank to slide on. *Otter* families seem to do this for recreation. Whether mud or snow, *otters* slide on both.

Skunks are also members of the *mink* family. Some folks comment that they aren't very smart. You don't have to be, if you have a pistol loaded with the kind of perfume that these boys carry! Very young *skunks* will mimic the adults in the correct position: facing the adversary, standing on the hands, tail up. Most people have a negative outlook on *skunks*, yet it's hard not to be taken by a mom *skunk* with a train of skunklets following along behind her as they go on foray for *insects*, *bird*'s eggs, and other edibles.

22. From Mountaintop and by River to the Sea

Mount Carleton and the associated hills are the roof of New Brunswick. At the modest height of 820 meters, Mt. Carleton is the highest point, not only in New Brunswick but in the whole of the Maritimes. Eons ago we had jagged mountains in our region that equaled for height the young (geologically) Rockies we have now. What we have here now are time-worn elevations with character. They are picturesque.

Mount Carleton's peak is not above the tree line. It's currently treeless, though, because of a fire in the 1920's and subsequent erosion, which washed the soil away. The summit has been reduced to an earlier successional stage, and it'll be a long way into the future before it is fully forested again, if ever.

Besides being a great place to visit (by foot is recommended), *Mt. Carleton* and its associated peaks of *Mount Head, Sagamook Mountain* and further to the east *Mount Elizabeth*, demonstrate the ecotone effect. This term refers to the flora and fauna living in a particular community that exhibits its own local climate, or micro-climate. *Thrushes* are good markers to illustrate this.

The veery inhabits the moist, shady alder and poplar stands at the bottom of the mountain. The name "veery" is a way of putting into words the song of this monochrome brown-coloured bird.

Going upslope among the larger birches and maples, and still with quite favourable micro-climate, we find the *wood thrush*. It's strongly spotted on the breast, and being the largest of the woodland *thrushes*, it's close to the bulk of the *robin*. To most ears, it has one of the most beautifully phrased songs of any North American bird.

As we climb (and remember that our base elevation was about 1000 ft.) we note some *fir* and *spruce* joining the *birches* and *maples*. Different parts of this ecotone are shared by two common *thrushes*. Where scattered tall trees stand above the others, we will likely find the sentinel singer, the *hermit thrush*. Where the trees are more uniform in size, and growing thickly, it'll be the *Swainson thrush*, which was formerly called the *olive-backed thrush*. These *Swainsons* are relatively easy to separate from the *hermit* as the latter has a distinctly rusty tail when compared to the mid-tone brown of its back.

When we leave the last *Swainsons* and *hermits* we're approaching the ecotone of a very habitat-restricted *thrush*. The smallish *Bicknell's* prefers the cool tops of the Central Highlands. It's a shy fellow, often using as a song post the interior of a bushy *black spruce* crown.

On a number of occasions, I've left the warm and sunny base to hear the wheezy song of the Bicknell's in a cold mist near the top of *Mt. Carleton* or *Sagamook*. The *Bicknell's* is an ornithologist's delight, considering its rarity and the skill required to differentiate it from the slightly larger, more widespread *gray-cheeked thrush*.

Before we leave the beauty of the peaks and head down one of the many rivers that rise in the *Highlands*, it's appropriate to consider the variety of wildlife present in this most remote area of the province. The *Highlands* is where the last woodland *caribou* known in New Brunswick lingered. It's also the core range of the *marten* and its larger relative the *fisher*. It's a likely spot for the *Canada lynx*; *black bears* are common here. It's exciting, too, that  *golden eagles*, observed in summer, may actually nest in the area. Big and Little Bald and Mount Elizabeth have been and are being watched for this activity.

If you're going to pick a stream to trace, there are many choices; water from the Highlands flows to all points of the compass. One could go north on the Upsalquitch; east down the Nipisiquit (meaning angry waters in the Micmac language); west on the Little Tobique, and eventually on the main Tobique; or south past Mount St. Nicholas in the Christmas Mountains and down the tumultuous North Pole Stream to the Little Southwest (Miramichi). The falls on Falls Brook on the main S.W. Miramichi is one of the Province's highest at 125 feet. Another remarkable falls is in Walton Glen on the Little Salmon River on the Fundy Shore. It's in the 200 foot range but isn't totally a free fall. All these water ways are avenues to the sea, which is the ultimate goal and destination of all waters.

Most streams rising in the Highlands have rocky beds and flow through forest. Further south in the province, streams are more placid, flanked by *alder* beds, reed marshes and bogs. Whatever stretch you happen to choose, and if you go by canoe, you'll have close to fabulous views of wildlife. Some likely sightings: *white-tailed does* and their *fawns*, *beavers*, *muskrats*, circling *ospreys* and *eagles*, families of *common mergansers*, and channel patrolling *kingfishers*. From early June to well into July, *warbler* and *vireo* songs will compete for your attention with the rattling of the moving water. Sometimes, early in the day when it's calm, birdsong can be almost deafening. A pleasant experience though!

The Main S.W. Miramichi at Juniper has a feature locally called the Alderground, well named and a great spot to fish for "*brookies*" (*brook trout*). There are some fine peat bogs in this area. Technically they'd be classified as domed, or higher in the centre, kind of reverse to the idea of a lake in a depression being gradually in-filled with *sphagnum*. This latter type happens too. Three pink flowered *orchids* are possible in these wild windswept places; calapogon, rose pogonia, and calypso. Insect eating plants are well placed in the bogs, where clouds of mosquitoes and other biters tend to temper the pleasure of being in such places for very long. *Pitcher plants*, *sundews* and *bladder worts* make a good living in the summer.

 Most of the expansive river marshes on the St. John River system are between Fredericton and Saint John City. Most are above the influence of salt water, even though the effect of tide is felt 90 miles upstream from the harbour. The marsh at Hampton is brackish. It's very productive of many species of *ducks, common snipe,* and *long-legged waders.*

23. Heroes and Heroines
of the Past

A female called Martha was the last of the *passenger pigeons*. She died alone in the Cinncinnati Zoo in 1914. These birds were once so abundant that flocks darkened the skies over much of North America. Nicholas Denys reported great flocks passing over what is now Miramichi City in June, 1650. The smallest flocks numbered 500 or 600 birds. Only five birds were reported at Point Lepreau on August 19, 1886. In 1899, a single bird at Scotch Lake north of Fredericton was the last of its kind reported in New Brunswick.

We were involved in the fate of two other species of birds as well.

The *Labrador duck*, so-called, was in low numbers in the 1850's. It's not certain whether it actually nested along the coast of Labrador. Not much is known of this duck. The drake was a striking black and white bird. The species favoured sandy estuaries, and wintered along the Atlantic seaboard from Long Island to Chesapeake Bay. The last one in New Brunswick was collected at Grand Manan by Simon Cheney, in April, 1871. (Cheney Island off Ignall's Head is named for the Cheney family.) No *Labrador ducks* were ever observed after 1875.

The other bird is the *Eskimo curlew*. Once abundant, it was the target of relentless shooting, especially during the 40 year period between 1850 and 1890. It was relatively easy to shoot, as it was trusting and allowed close approach, and flew in compact flocks. It was blasted both in the spring and fall. Gunners hauled away their take by the wagon load. The onslaught took its toll, and by 1929 ornithologists thought this bird was extinct. Up to the new millenium, however, there are still scattered reports of a few individuals at a time. A report of a flock of 23 in Texas in May, 1981 caused a flurry among birders.

A sister species is the *little curlew* of Siberia, which doesn't have a large population. They were regularly seen in fall migration from August to mid-September up to the 1890's on the peat barrens of Miscou, in parties of up to 75 individuals. This was their favourite resort in N.B.

If you look at the mammals in any given region, it seems that larger and more ferocious carnivores are the ones most likely to be persecuted. We followed that principle here in New Brunswick with wolves, and it worked. A bounty passed by the legislature in 1792 allowed the payment of 20 shillings for each wolf over one year in age. They were shot, trapped and poisoned so that by 1900 they were scarce. Even so, they were still quite common in the 1840's, as a grandmother living in rural Carleton County, walking between her neighbour's house and her own at dusk, had a pack of at least six jump off a bank and run along the roadway ahead of her. Initially she thought they were sheep. It was only when they turned tail and ran off that she realized they were wolves. Later she commented that they "were quite inoffensive - not fierce at all!" The last confirmed wolf was sighted in the Salmon River watershed near Chipman in 1901. Our coyote is the largest of its kind. So, once again, Mother Nature puts in a replacement that' s almost like the original!

There are questions about the *cougar*. Did we ever have it? Do we have it now? Will we have this, the largest wild felid in North America, in the future? Writing in the 1950's wildlife biologist Bruce Wright became famous trying to document the presence of this super predator in this Province. Most authorities didn't believe him. As to the future, *cougars* have been confirmed as close as Pennsylvania and the Gaspe, as recently as late 2002. *Cougars* prefer the *white-tailed deer* as prey, so if our deer herd diminishes it's not likely that they'll move in.

Next down in size from the *cougar* is the *Canada lynx*. It is now present in significant numbers only in the north of the province, in the Campbellton/Bathurst area.

As to the *black bear*, even with spring sports hunting they seem to be holding their own at about 6000 animals estimated for the whole province. The bear seems to be able to "accommodate" man in its life style. It's unfortunate, though, that a lot of them are "spoiled," or garbage *bears*. Without bear-proof garbage containers, or with sloppy handling of offal, they will continue to be a problem.

We once had three kinds of *deer* roaming the forests and wildlands of New Brunswick. One, the beautiful *caribou*, the woodland race, has been gone since the mid-1930's. They have been partly pushed out by the *white-tail*, not physically but subtly, by being infected by a brain worm parasite that is passive in the deer but fatal to the *caribou*, and sometimes fatal to the *moose*. The alternate host is a common *snail*. The *caribou* had other problems: it was good to eat, travelled in small herds, was not very wary and was therefore easy to shoot. Forest change from old growth to younger age classes no doubt had an effect too. The nearest population of *woodland caribou* currently is on the mountains of the Gaspe Peninsula.

Our populations of two important raptors have taken a turn for the better. The low point was the 1970's for both the *bald eagle* and the *peregrine falcon*. The once highly lauded insecticide, DDT, was eventually implicated. It caused sterility, egg-shell thinning, and other negative effects. Raising and releasing young *falcons* (it's called "hacking") helped the *peregrine*. The *bald eagle* did its own recovery, with a reduction in persecution and new food sources from aquaculture and the commercial fishery helping. Placing animal carcasses and butchery leftovers out in open areas during the critical winter period is helping the adults that stay resident year 'round. Three cheers for both these magnificent raptors.

A short posthumous tribute to
Bruce Wright, Wildlife Biologist

Bruce Wright spent much energy during his professional career, and while head of the Northeastern Wildlife Station in Fredericton, trying to prove once and for all the existence of the Eastern panther or cougar within the boundaries of New Brunswick. He was altruistic in documenting literally hundreds of sight records from every section of the province, though he himself had never seen what has proven to be a most elusive beast. During his working years he produced as solo author two books and many articles on his quest. His critics claimed he fanned the embers of excitement when the fire should have been allowed to quietly smoulder out. Yet there was redemption for Bruce. When he was retired and terminally ill, his wife Marjorie invited him to join her for a drive through quiet country roads in their beloved Stanley area. Lo and behold, a cougar streaked across the road. Bruce was at last content.

24. An Evening Chorus to End the Day and the Play

We started this book with an early morning chorus in the early spring along a stream and in the newly leaved woods. For an evening chorus let's gather around a campfire on a beach in mid-July. Behind the beach there's a steep, sloping hardwood ridge.

As we sit around on flat rocks, we hear the repeated phrases of the *red-eyed vireo*: "Here I am. I see you. Do you see me?" Pretty constant too is the cu cu cu in threes and fours, the trademark of the *black-billed cuckoo*. The cuckoo seems to be thanking the powers that be for a good supply of hairy *tent caterpillars*, a preferred food. As the sun drops to the horizon, if we listen we will hear the clear pleasant notes of the *vesper sparrow*. Trees at the top of the beach screen the field he's singing from, but we feel sure he's using a favourite fence rail as a song post.

Dusk is now imminent. A *robin* scolds as he lands near our little party. A *spotted sandpiper* goes "peet, peet, weet," as she flies past on stiff, short-stroke wings. Her year's young aren't airborne yet and scurry into cover further up the beach. Out over the calm water, *tree* and *barn swallows* swoop and spin, feeding on flies of all kinds. In the water there's a great lunge near shore. Striped bass – a salmon would have come clear of the water's surface. From a side pond a tentative trill identifies a tardy *toad*; tardy because at this time it should have been in somebody's garden. Old chug-a-rum, the *green frog*, is staying until the last of the light disappears.

From the full-crowned hardwoods, a few measured notes of a *wood thrush* reach our ears, recalling Henry Wadsworth Longfellow's *And where the shadows deepest fell, The wood thrush rang his silver bell*. This thrush is certainly one of our top songsters. It was Thoreau who said he found this bird's song most genial to his own nature.

As we break out the marshmallows, further along the shore, where a few large *red spruce* join the *maples* and *yellow birches*, we can make out the faint, flute-like phrases of a *mint hermit thrush*. Its song is offered again in a few minutes; "the evening belongs to the *thrushes*." *Warblers*, in contrast, sing more vigorously in the morning, so it's a treat to pick up an *ovenbird* serenade, a glittering warble given on the wing. This is a bird that spends most of its waking hours among the leaves on the forest floor.

Just as we thought we had heard the last of the forest bird music for the evening, the clear tinkling notes, ecstatic in delivery, of a *winter wren* come from a point higher on the ridge, in the vicinity of a babbling brook. A check with a second hand gave the length of the uninterrupted offering: 10 amazing seconds.

By now it's becoming quite dark. More fish jump. Their identity can't even be guessed at. A *woodcock* buzzes over our fire with short, quick wing beats, its dumpy body and extra long bill silhouetted against the sky, now brightened by a rising moon, near full. A couple of little *brown bats* swoop low over the water near the shore. They're taking over the work of the swallows. These strong-flying bats are joined by a smaller one with a weak, almost moth-like, flight, probably an *eastern pipistrelle*. All the *bats* disappear when a pair of *common nighthawks* come to fly around in circles, only the white flashes in their wings clearly visible. Their actions are punctuated by harsh, nasal "peent" calls.

Suddenly from the nearby trees the long clear whistles of "Sweet, Canada, Canada, Canada," drift down to us. Someone comments jokingly, "That's the little gray bird that sings in the night!" More specifically, the *white-throated sparrow*. A very abundant and much-loved New Brunswicker.

As we fold our blankets and gather up the picnic gear for the trek home to the old farmhouse, we're accompanied by scattered *fire flies*. From the same hardwood ridge where the thrushes were earlier, we hear the "who cooks for you" and "who cooks for you allllllllllll" of the *barred owl*. Suddenly, a deeper-voiced one answers from further down the ridge. We're going to have a duet. This is too good to pass up, and for the next 20 minutes or so, we listen to their laughs, barks, and crying sounds. They turn it all on, capping for us a night to remember.

Useful References

Here are a couple of useful references that are current:

1. Christie, David S. et al: "Birds of New Brunswick: An Annotated List", the New Brunswick Museum, Saint John, NB, 2004   Cost $15.00

2. Hinds, Harold R., "Flora of New Brunswick", 2nd edition, the University of New Brunswick, Fredericton, New Brunswick, 2004   Cost $50.00

For a helpful map of many of the region's larger parks and recreation areas, pick up any local road map of New Brunswick

About the Author

Hank Deichmann holds a BSc in Forestry from UNB and has done course work toward the MSc in Wildlife Biology from Acadia. As a child, he spent countless hours wandering the fields, woods, and shores of the Kingston Peninsula in New Brunswick, which left him with an insatiable curiosity about nature. As a consequence, he pursued a variety of outdoor-oriented careers, most notably the position of Chief Interpreter and Ecologist with Parks Canada, Atlantic Region. His writing appears in a number of regional magazines and newspapers.